T0067228

From
CHOICES
—— *Come* ——
CHANGE

F K LANSDOWNE

BALBOA
PRESS

A DIVISION OF HAY HOUSE

Copyright © 2018 F K LANSDOWNE.

All rights reserved. No part of this book may be used or reproduced by
any means, graphic, electronic, or mechanical, including photocopying,
recording, taping or by any information storage retrieval system
without the written permission of the author except in the case of
brief quotations embodied in critical articles and reviews.

Balboa Press books may be ordered through booksellers or by contacting:

Balboa Press
A Division of Hay House
1663 Liberty Drive
Bloomington, IN 47403
www.balboapress.com
1 (877) 407-4847

Because of the dynamic nature of the Internet, any web addresses or
links contained in this book may have changed since publication and
may no longer be valid. The views expressed in this work are solely those
of the author and do not necessarily reflect the views of the publisher,
and the publisher hereby disclaims any responsibility for them.

The author of this book does not dispense medical advice or prescribe the use
of any technique as a form of treatment for physical, emotional, or medical
problems without the advice of a physician, either directly or indirectly. The
intent of the author is only to offer information of a general nature to help
you in your quest for emotional and spiritual well-being. In the event you use
any of the information in this book for yourself, which is your constitutional
right, the author and the publisher assume no responsibility for your actions.

Any people depicted in stock imagery provided by Getty Images are
models, and such images are being used for illustrative purposes only.
Certain stock imagery © Getty Images.

Print information available on the last page.

ISBN: 978-1-5043-9408-6 (sc)
ISBN: 978-1-5043-9410-9 (hc)
ISBN: 978-1-5043-9409-3 (e)

Library of Congress Control Number: 2017919299

Balboa Press rev. date: 04/05/2018

CONTENTS

TO BEGIN

In the beginning was the word and in the end there will be silence.

Not fiction but fact, the way it was always intended with or without the help of mankind. For it was always the intention to show mankind the way forward. Always the intention of many to be beacons of light, to show the way to anyone who would listen. To listen and to learn, realising that there is far more to life than what is seen or perceived to be around them.

Something that cannot be fully explained by the human mind for it is something so incredible, so complex that it is far beyond any form that exists on this planet. A life force, so advanced from anything known to man that anything so far explained by scientists is only a tiny scratch on the surface of comprehension of ALL THAT IS.

ALL THAT IS, being the totality of the universe one that we are part of, a fragment but still an important fragment just the same. Each of us playing our roles in life like players on the stage. Each one of us knowingly or unknowingly playing out the roles we came to play on our journey. Our life's experience in the human form on this chosen planet - this time. Chosen from a state of our being - in our natural form. One which is 1,000,000 miles from here and yet - isn't. One that can be transformed from in a nanosecond if so desired.

A journey that takes just an instant from one form of energy to another as we know it in the human mind. It is something that I cannot explain to you fully, it comes from a place of knowing, one of being in tune with something so magnificent and so wondrous. A place that is open to all of us and is used daily in our lives either consciously or unconsciously, with intention or used without the slightest thought about where or how certain things have happened, transpired or miraculously come about. A force and power so great and yet normally cannot be seen by the human eye. Some can and see different forms of energy in relation to what they are open to, what they have previously used or what powers they have bought with them as tools to do the job they came here to do.

So here I am coming to you in this form to help you and guide you if you so desire, to have a greater understanding of yourself and the universe in which you live. It is simply a choice and not one that is foisted upon anyone at any time, as the universe is about love and free will. So for you to take steps towards a better understanding is purely down to you.

For there are no laws that you must do anything or be anyone at all. Everything is of your own choosing from the moment you enter this life and from the moment you depart - but I will go into that later. At the moment for you to have a better understanding of yourself and the universe is more important, than to go into any depths of the whys and wherefores.

It is this moment that is paramount, for that is all we ever have. Yesterday is purely memory and tomorrow - well it is yet to be written. For anything can be changed in a instant if we so desire it to be. Not in the material sense of change but in the way we react and also our perception to all that is around us. To be open to other people's way of thinking; as quite often their view of how things are, are quite different to our own.

Think of it as a circle, where everyone is standing on the perimeter looking in. Everyone's view will be different because they are looking at whatever it is in question, from a different standpoint.

The same can be said of a different point of view because each of us have come from a different beginning. Each had a different upbringing and the circumstances and views for everyone will be different. It cannot be any other way for everything and everyone is unique in every possible way.

So what is it that you would like to change in your life or indeed the world?

Maybe more of this and more of that?

That will make no difference at all in the long run. It is to be a peace with what is and then look to see how and where you would like a difference to be made, either spiritually or indeed materially. More of anything just for the sake of having more is not the answer but purely a sweetener to postpone the moment of taking responsibility and making sometimes that much-needed change.

So we are on a journey are we not? A journey of discovery of who and what we are. A journey unique to each and every one of us, no matter what our race, religion or creed. A widening of a circle that you are already in, some call it the circle of life and in many ways it is. Only the circle of life can be broken, stepped out of or expanded in the most glorious way, when we are ready to accept change of any kind, albeit in a thought, word or deed. Then and only then will things be different and move on to something new, if that is the intention. For the power to change things whether they be for better or for worse, lies squarely in our own hands. We have free will, for that is what is intended and what each of us has been given. To do and be what we wish to be - there are exceptions and in fact exceptions to everything.

Later, much later, to grasp the fundamentals first is the key to change.

So to make changes, you first need to know what it is you would like to change in your life or your present situation, which is not always as clear as it may seem. It may be in the form of a relationship, where you live or the work you do, in fact a whole host of things. Knowing how to make those changes or understanding why you are indeed in your current situation is a whole different matter.

Being where you are at this moment in time is precisely where you put yourself, either by circumstances or by choice, and even in given circumstances you still have a choice. You make choices continuously throughout your day, from food, the people you meet and the places you choose to go. Everything is a choice and by making these choices you are creating your day.

From choices comes change in every shape and form. Just as you choose what to wear each day; it's all the same thing. How are you feel about yourself, how you wish others to see you and respond to you, it all comes down to choice.

To make changes - if you do not like what you have now, this is to start choosing differently in everything that you do. It is more complex than just choosing differently but it is a start, if that is what you wish to do. No good saying if only this or that would happen in my life, it is up to each individual to decide what it is they would like to alter and taking the appropriate steps to bring that about. Sometimes it takes courage and determination to make these changes. At other times it only takes a simple change of thought to implement it. It really all depends what it is of course. Some things are harder than others, some are very subtle and hardly noticeable until you look back and notice the difference, others have to be implemented overtime because they are so great that they take a while to put into place and also for you to adjust to them.

Many people are opposed to change, wanting everything to stay the same, so they surround themselves with all that is known and familiar, and dare I say fear anything that is unfamiliar to them. At some point though they will change as everything does. To resist is futile, for the universe is all about change, evolving, growing and forever moving forwards to something fresh and new.

So why would some people resist?

Some to avoid confrontation, others think they would be letting others down in some way or perhaps being in a family that has always done things a certain way and they do not wish to upset the status quo. To be different or to think they have a duty to follow their wishes instead of their own.

It is not about what others are doing or being in this life but what you are doing and being. This is the most important thing of all, for not being you and all you stand for is denying the opportunity for you to grow. Being what someone else wants you to be and not being you is missing the opportunity given to you by the circumstances you find yourself in.

This book will give you the guidance and many insights into the reasons why you are here and also ways in which you can move forward into a more fulfilling and purposeful life, if that as I said, is your desire. There will be many insights to in the workings of the universe and opportunities to grasp the realisation of life itself. How you use this book and view this knowledge is entirely up to you. It is purely a choice and free will.

A BRAND NEW DAY

One in which you can change the direction of your life and the circumstances that you live in if they are such that you wish to change them.

First a time of contemplation, time out if you can alone, away from all the hustle and bustle of everyday life - well normally. Somewhere peaceful and tranquil, somewhere you feel comfortable, it can be anywhere. A favourite chair, the garden, a place you like to go. Just somewhere where you can reflect without any interference of any kind. If you are inside then turning off phone and mobile for a short while. Now try and review your life from an outsider, as though you were looking in on yourself. Completely detached from circumstances and make a mental note of the things that come to mind - try and keep away from the monetary issues at this point for that is something to deal with later.

For you to be a peace at this particular moment is of paramount importance. To still your mind if you can and detach from all of that is around you. See if you can pinpoint what your main concerns are, writing them down as they come to mind is very helpful.

Bringing them to the surface like this, is the easiest way that I know of to bring - sometimes hidden agendas and issues to the fore. Writing them down brings them into the realm of the tangible instead of being something in the subconscious. As long as the intention is to be still and silent, that is all that is required. Business disrupts the flow. Most times it is a thought that will come to mind giving you guidance and a direction that you previously had not thought of. Any clarity given will always be helpful. A direction that can be explored if you so choose or indeed dismissed. As I cannot say enough - it is always your choice, always your decision. The direction you take in life is always your choice and responsibility - ALWAYS.

Another way to find solace and direction is to be amongst nature. Nature being the purest form of energy that there is on this planet, one that sustains you, feeds you and purifies the air around you. One that clears the senses, brings peace and calmness to the mind, which of course has been known for thousands of years but needs to be bought back to our attention now and again. As so often it is these simplest of things that get pushed out our daily routines by the continuous need to be busy. Blocking out all natural communication and all the natural things that are so essential to our well-being. Yet most times it is the last thing we think of doing, unless we get the point of exhaustion and feeling so tired that we have to stop and take a much needed rest. It really should not be this way, an enforced rest or break, but something that is done on a daily basis. Not moments taken to sit in front of the television or the computer or out on the town to have a few drinks to relax. No this is not what is meant by taking time out for you.

A time for just sitting quietly having a moments peace even if only for ten minutes in a day. Just this short time would be most beneficial if practiced daily. A time of reflection a time to just be.

Being at peace is something we all should be aiming for in our everyday lives, even if we do not like the situation that we are in. It is to be at peace with what is in your life at this present time but also taking the necessary steps to change what it is that you wish to change.

It is possible to have a very busy schedule and still be at peace, if you are indeed enjoying what you are doing. Whether it be in the workplace, home, sports or anything that you participate in. It is about choosing carefully what is right for you and whether it uplifts you or makes you feel heavy. If it is the latter then please if you can leave it alone and find an alternative, as anything without joy is something to be avoided whenever possible.

Joy in your life is one of life's greatest pleasures, so if it is lacking in any area of your life whether it be friendship, work, where you live or anything at all which does not feel comfortable, then it is up to you and no one else to change whatever it is as soon as you can or as soon as it is possible. Depending on what it is and how easy it is to change. Some things are easier than others, with say a friendship then an end to it sooner than later is best.

In the case of work or home for instance then it may take many months or even sometimes even a year or two to bring about. It very much depends on the situation and what you are willing to do about it. If you think the situation will get better of its own accord and just go away, then in most cases you would be wrong. There are exceptions to everything. Sometimes just changing the way you are to people or having a different perspective on something will change things completely without having to physically do anything. There are not many occasions though that this is so. Most changes take courage, determination and the willingness to see them through. It is for us to be responsible both for our actions and our choices as anything we choose shapes our future.

We came into this world on our own and it is for us, and us predominantly to choose how we live, how we act, and indeed how we are to others around us. It is no good us saying I would have done so-and-so, if it wasn't for some other person. This is not being responsible and not being who we are. For us to be accountable for our own actions and no one else's is of paramount importance to our well-being. What anyone else is doing, or being is of little importance.

It is for you to be all you can be regardless of what is going on around you. The courage to be you, the courage to be a unique individual that you are in every possible way. It is to detach yourself from any given situation and ask yourself - Is this who I truly am? Not to go on regardless without consideration of what you are doing or being.

Being, is what I will explain more fully later on. But for now, doing is some form of action and being 'is one of being' the real you. One of being responsible for all of your actions.

Whatever your situation or position you hold in this life makes no difference in the scheme of things spiritually. We are all here having a human experience. Each of us on our own unique journey, it is only our reaction to our experiences that makes the difference overall. The position held really is irrelevant, although from a human viewpoint, all the difference in the world some would say.

It does seem rather odd when you look at how much some people have and then others who have very little. Some being given it seems every opportunity in life and others very little. Some cruising through life without so much as a care in the world, whilst others strive for survival. Having to make ends meet in the way of resources, even being born in the poorest of circumstances. These are all circumstances which people have chosen from their spiritual state in which to live out the life, lessons and experiences for this lifetime.

Now this may seem very odd and unbelievable too many people. How can this possibly be?

It is because we are essentially spirit and not the human form some would take us to be. Spirit having a human experience - experiencing human form, a tangible existence for while. To experience themselves differently. Even we do that from time to time, well most of us. Going to countries other than our own to have 'a different experience'. One perhaps of a culture change or one of a physical adventure. Sensing and feeling different sensations, tastes and traditions. Learning a new skill, all kinds of activities. All enhancing our journey called life.

Well from a soul perspective we are doing the same kind of thing - experiencing. Only from a human viewpoint does it seem at times a very long journey. In the life of a spirit though, it is only a blip in our existence. To open your minds to something much greater than what you see around you is to open your mind to a greater understanding of yourself as a whole, the world and the universe that you are a part as we are spirit in essence and unique in every possible way.

If you can accept or even suppose there could be more to life than what you see around you, then you have taken the first step on the way to discovering a new truth about yourself. One that will enable you, if you so choose to unlock certain aspects about yourself that have previously been unknown to you. When you have the information to hand that this book gives you, then all kinds of changes and transformations can take place. It is this knowing that you are far more than is seen by human eye.

Showing you that you can change your life for the better in almost every way. As long as you have the courage and determination to make the changes desired. How and when this happens is entirely down to you. Each of us has our own agenda, our own journeys to follow or indeed change at some point. Change they will voluntarily or otherwise in the course of time, but to do it sooner rather than have a situation forced upon you is indeed is a far more desirable way to proceed.

The whole universe and the world is about change, hopefully for the better. Well that is always the intention and always will be. It is up to us though to implement such changes in any way that we can. That unfortunately is not always the outcome, as many many things have still to be learnt in this world, recognised as such and moved on from. Far too many to list here but are gone into in detail further on in this book.

Eventually all will be revealed in relation to you in your world, as far as would be appropriate for now. Any more than that would do more harm than good. It is what you can use in your world at this present time that is important. So let's make an effort to broaden our minds to something that is both beneficial to your life not only in this lifetime but in the next also. How greatly you benefit is entirely down to you. How great your problems are that you wish to fix if any, and how willing and open you are to suggestions, trusting your inner guidance. Open to being you, the unique person that you are and having the courage and conviction to change what it is that brings you to reading this book. As it is no coincidence, that I assure you.

All things are created; either by ourselves and what we have desired or like now created by the universe to try and help where ever it can, without interfering in anyway with the free will that you always have and will always have. How you can change things will become apparent to you from the many ways given to you in this book. Your situation, your life and you are unique to you. Although in many ways similar to other people's problems as in relationships, work, illness and the like, but still never totally the same ever.

Why is it we need this help? Because the world is rapidly becoming one of dependency and people believing that they are unable to do things for themselves. Believing it is all in the hands of experts in various fields and feeling that they have no power to do or change anything for the better. There are some people making vast changes for a better world but in this book I am talking of the majority of the world as a whole, and not the few who already realise the impact of seeing what is real and truly meaningful and what is not. It is for me to try and lead you to a place of understanding and in ways that will help you understand the world and the universe around you better.

It is simply not of being born into this world, growing up, working, retiring and leaving this earthly plain. It is far far more than that and for you to be a part of that bigger picture is my aim. Not that you are not part of it already, you are. But to be consciously aware of it and work with it, is something that will benefit you greatly.

Sometimes it is only the doubts that you have in yourself and of the universe that holds you back.

THE BIGGER PICTURE

Eventually, everything reverts back to its natural state, whether it be plants, living creatures, human beings or inanimate objects.

In the beginning were atoms and particles, we to are those atoms and particles, indeed, everything you see, feel and touch is and will always remain so. How wondrous is that?

Amazing to think that so much can be created from so little, so intricate so colourful and all so perfect in its own way. Something so complex, and so wondrous, and yet we hardly give it a thought about how this is possible, or indeed how this could possibly be. When you think of how many billions and trillions of different things there are in the world, each with it own function, each having its own purpose, an endless array of wonderment. An endless array of joy too, if only we would allow it to be so.

There comes a time in man's evolvement, when it is appropriate to take a pause, a moment to reflect all that is before you, and to seek answers to all that is questionable, to all that is unspeakable, and to seek answers on how all this can possibly be.

Just look at leaf or flower and comprehend all its complexities, from its infinite beginning to its glorious unfoldment.

How can the seed that drops to the ground and takes root grow into a beautiful tree from just a small seed?

How can all that intelligence be in that one little seed? Knowing exactly when the conditions are right, how to grow, how to produce branches, leaves, bark, in fact, everything perfectly and so naturally in its own way, all from that one tiny little seed.

An amazing feat by Mother Nature, doesn't it make you wonder? Is it not worth a moment's thought, a moment of consideration of how all this can be?

Yes a time of self-discovery, a time to reflect all that is before you.

To those of you who doubt the sincerity of these words, I ask you now to just consider them and not throw them out because they seem unfamiliar to you. Just because they are different from what has gone before does not make them inappropriate now, and just because you cannot feel, touch or see something, does not mean it is not there. In fact, there is more in the unseen, than there is in the tangible that you feel, touch, see and use in your every day environment.

You use a cell phone every day and take for granted the connection and to be able to communicate between one side of the world to the other, yet you cannot see the airwaves that enable you to do this. Or isn't it rather remarkable the speed in which the connection is made even thousands and thousands of miles apart.

All I am asking is for you to open your minds to something much bigger, much grander than anything you have ever known or that has gone before. It is time now in man's evolution to have a better understanding of themselves and of the universe in which they live, and not to think of themselves as the only living species in the universe, as after all, the universe is a vastly immense place. To imagine even that we are the only living species is to be blinkered from all possibilities and opportunities for us all to grow, both in mind and in spirit.

We use things in our everyday lives, that we cannot see, without a second thought, and it seems very natural for us to do so, so how wonderful would it be to use what we cannot see in other wonderful and natural ways to.

Your computer is quite happy to run off something that cannot be seen, it draws in data and e-mails, pictures even, so why not us? Yet you do it at an unconscious level every day, with every thought, sudden moment of inspiration, talents and creativity of every kind without a moment's hesitation. So if this can be achieved at an unconscious level, why not through the power of conscious thought and intent.

You see, you draw towards you, those moments of inspiration and many other gifts - from you would say thin air, but this thin air contains all the data, information and creativity that you will ever need. It is there for you to use and draw upon, it's about opening your mind to it.

Children learn to do this at a very early age and have such wonderful imaginations; some are encouraged to nurture those imaginations, whilst other children are told not to have such flights of fantasy. It is in these times of imagination, or flights of fantasy that much can be achieved to broaden the mind and realise that anything is possible if we only put our minds to it. When I say mind to it, it is a thought process. A thought put into action becomes a reaction to that thought, giving it the power to become a reality in your world. So you see the imagination and thought process is a very powerful and empowering thing, if encouraged at an early age can lead onto many great achievements.

For as a child you dream of what you would like to be as you get older. These dreams are not fanciful, but are to lead you onto what you really came here to do and be, to suppress these dreams, can quite often lead to a loss of direction in one's life.

It is only by going deep within oneself can you rediscover this lost self the real you, your ultimate life's journey, your life's path and purpose. A question as I said earlier, of peeling back the layers of your past, until you find the real you and all you came on this planet do and to achieve. Not to leave it until your twilight years to reflect and think back on all you could have been, the missed opportunities, the if only's and the I wish I had done!'

Life is an adventure to be lived and to be enjoyed, not just for some of us but for all of us.

We all come on chosen paths and journeys; it is up to each one of us to be all we can be in this world and beyond. Each on our own journey, whatever that might be, it does not matter what he, she or it is doing, but what you are doing. It is about your journey on this planet that matters, a question of focus, courage and the determination to see your dreams flourish and grow. A question of love, not only to yourself but to others, and to the planet that sustains you.

Whenever there is a conflict between the soul and the human mind, there is an imbalance that needs to be addressed within the framework of our experience here on earth. Something that is essential if we are to grow as spirits, and also attain our true potential here in this reality.

To be out of balance with who we truly are is neither helpful or advantageous to our growth, for it is in this growth that we evolve, and without this growth there can be no expansion either in this world or the next. Swimming without motion I would call it, and what's the point in that.

Whenever there is conflict in the body caused by stress, or some other underlying issue, it has a tendency to reveal itself in a variety of different forms. Some in an obvious fashion as in a growth or tumour and also in other less obvious ways as in constant headaches, backache and the more life threatening diseases such as cancer and other blood related disorders. All these and more (not always), can be a direct link to stress, environmental issues, diet and lifestyle or a whole combination of the above. The 'cure' usually associated with all of these rests with the beholder of the said malaise or imbalance.

It's not just a matter of treating the disease or ailment, or cutting out the affected part but of treating the imbalance at its core and the reason behind the ailment, as these things don't just happen. There is nearly always a cause, and the cause always has an effect.

There are many instances when treating the disease or cutting out the affected part is the only way to prolong life. But once this is done, it is still of great urgency to get to the core of the problem and the reason of the ailment in the first place, therein treating the whole of the condition and not just the outcome of the said cause. To not treat the cause of the problem is to leave it to possibly return and manifest again, or sometimes to return in other forms.

It is a time to reflect on one's life, a time to make some much-needed adjustments, not a punishment as so many people would have you believe. That is why so many people who have had life-threatening diseases make radical changes in their lives, they turn a corner and realise indeed that it was a gift - a chance to do things differently, an opportunity to make a fresh start.

To treat the illness is wonderful, but it does not take away the core of the problem, the reason in the first place for the malaise.

Treating the symptom and not the cause is no permanent answer to the problem. There are so many medical drugs being taken, so many things to alleviate pain, when the pain is an indication as to where the problem lies. Just as with a cut or a similar kind of injury, the pain lets you know where the problem is. The fixing of the problem can be quite complex sometimes, and not just a case of putting a plaster over a cut, sometimes as with a serious injury it takes longer to heal.

It depends on the nature of the problem and the severity of the illness or malaise. There are many factors to take into account, and undoubtedly a question of when the first symptoms began.

Sometimes, a complex process, but well worth the effort and courage it entails. A change in one's lifestyle perhaps,? Whatever it is, it will always be a change for the better. A positive change that can bring many benefits to the life in question.

There is an imbalance in our society, we have come too far away from a natural lifestyle and what was intended for us. A change of direction now is needed to correct this imbalance and to address the many issues over health and our general well-being, in terms of stress, diet, and much-needed relaxation. A time to take responsibility for whom and what we are and not waiting for someone else to do it for us!

It's up to each individual to make a difference, not only to their environment but to their own general well-being and health. It's not up to doctors and medical profession to keep you healthy, it's up to you to choose more consciously in what you eat and what you do. There is no point blaming manufacturers for what they put into your food, choose wisely, choose differently, nobody makes you buy it or eat it. Make healthier fresher food choices, your whole system will benefit greatly and so will your environment.

A conscious effort, a conscious change is all that is needed to turn the whole thing around. Do you really want your children, or grandchildren to grow up in a world that is becoming more and more dependent on medical drugs? In a world where relaxation and fresh food is almost a thing of the past, where it is getting increasingly difficult, to get peace and quiet, a time when anything natural is thought of as a thing of the past?

This time is approaching us fast, you may not even realise it but you only have to look back over the past two decades to know and see what I mean. Which does not mean to say that it was better then, but in respects of eating and relaxation, it certainly was.

To move forward in a conscious manner now is the way forward, to be ever mindful of what we are doing and being both to others and indeed ourselves. A change of perspective, a change of thought is all that is needed.

In every country the issues of life seem to be the same, one of dissatisfaction and discontent, whether it be about money, their looks or a complete dissatisfaction about who they are and what role they play in their life. Many not realising that they have chosen their given roles to play from a spiritual state before they were born into this world. A role they wished to experience and from a place chosen in which to learn the lessons that they came on this planet to learn.

A never-ending voyage of discovery to discover, who and what are you really about, an amazing array of choices to be made along the way. So why would you want to be anything other than what you have chosen yourself? Because it looks more attractive, that's why.

You have no way of knowing though where another's path is leading, or in fact why they have chosen their present role. We are all in different stages of our evolvement, we are by nature spirits, who have chosen in most cases, to experience life as a human being in the roles we have chosen and to experience.

We have also chosen to learn lessons, along with his experience, which enable us to grow and evolve as spirit. They may be lessons from an earlier experience or lifetime, something we had issues with or something that we avoided doing or being. It may even be an experience we gave others and need to learn from that experience by reliving it ourselves. For whatever reason or for whatever purpose, you are in the right body, you are in the right country, and you are living the life you chose. You may not like what you have chosen of course, in that case it is up to each individual to take responsibility for self and decide to choose differently from what you are doing and being.

Everyone has the opportunity to change their lives in some way, if only they have the courage and determination to do so. Even people from the humblest of surroundings and start in life have moved mountains in the way of moving their lives forward, through sheer determination and focus. They know from deep down, that they can better themselves and have focused mainly on their dreams, and how they can bring them to fruition. They have an unshakable faith, both in themselves and in the universe to deliver.

This drive and focus is not just in the underprivileged but in every one, it's just that their circumstance and surroundings gives them more drive if you like to do something positive about it.

In more comfortable surroundings, we are sometimes more inclined to go with the flow and not make the effort, but that is all part of our lesson in the grander scheme of things.

A divine scheme, where all 'is matter', a state of being, our natural state.

There are many reasons as to why people do not fulfil their dreams or attain their true potential in this lifetime. Many feel they cannot aspire to such heights and many simply do not make the effort. So many wish they had of course, when they get on in years, and sometimes even remember their dreams when it is too late and almost time to leave this earthly plane.

It is usually at this time that so many older people have regrets, look back on their lives and remember all the missed opportunities that were open to them. All the if only's come to light at this point, sometimes to much earlier on in years when people have the sudden realisation of what it is they have come to do.

If only they had the courage and commitment, the focus and determination, their lives would have been totally different from what they have experienced. So much more fulfilling, a feeling of contentment and achievement in so many ways. Not only in their experience of life but also in their health and well-being, not living out your dreams only stunts your growth not only in the physical but in the spiritual life too.

For you are spirit, we all are and I feel that has been mostly lost in today's lifestyle and the way we view ourselves and our surroundings.

Most of us have chosen to forget that we are spirit, and just live with the reality that they can see and touch around them, ignoring the complexities and the wonders of this planet, their lives and indeed the universe of which they are part. Detaching themselves from who they really are, and ignoring certain factors in their lives that are trying to steer them closer to their real selves, to who and what they are. The path they chose to experience on this planet, to the life experience they previously chose as spirit's before their arrival here.

Many see setbacks in their lives as obstacles to be overcome or some kind of punishment or have a 'why me' attitude to something that has befallen them. But I can tell you now, there is no such thing as a coincidence, there is no such thing as a punishment. Everything that happens in your life happens for a very good reason, even what you would consider to be your darkest hour, is there for a reason, there is a purpose and a reason for everything in your lives.

Sometimes a time of adjustment of some kind, a change of direction, a change of location, a change of relationships, even an accident or illness to stop you in your tracks. You may even have an insight into the reason at a later date when you look back at the time of the occurrence. It may even have been a case of losing your job and causing you hardship, offering you the chance to change jobs and direction, although I doubt it at the time whether you would see it in this way, and only see it as a setback.

It is down to you how you choose to view your present circumstances, and what steps you wish to take if any, to remedy the situation you see as so dire and sometimes life-threatening. The severity of the occurrence whatever it may be, will almost certainly be in line with how far off you are in this life's journey, and what you came to learn and experience.

So far away have many of us come from living a natural lifestyle, not only in what we think say or do, but in what we eat, drink or indeed put onto our bodies in ways that do ultimate harm and damage to our bodies, mental and spiritual states. Lotions and potions filled with chemicals that get absorbed into the system and into every part of our totality.

What is uplifting is the continued growth of natural creams, lotions and cosmetics on the market giving us a healthier choice for our skin and bodies, using naturally based ingredients from flowers and plants.

It is for us to choose differently and selectively if we wish for better health, a clearer mind and spirit, for all these things that we do are so unnatural and damaging. To choose wisely and be responsible for all our choices, whatever they may be.

It is a choice, you have free will to do and be as you please but are you truly happy with how you feel, what you are doing or being?

A TIME TO LEARN

In a world of ever decreasing optimism and where tales of doom and gloom are abound, it's hardly any wonder that people are turning to alcohol and other forms of stimulants to alleviate the feelings of despair and gloom, mostly brought about by a feeling that they're trapped perhaps or a feeling of inadequacy in not being able to improve their situation or their lives. Unless you are a child dependent on love and care from elders, then there is everything you can do to improve both your life and how you feel about it.

Too much negativity is portrayed. Just because something is printed or stated does not make it so, just because something printed is negative does not make it so, that is only their perspective. You can make up your own minds and view things differently if you so choose, for negativity attracts negativity, and likewise a sense of positivity will bring with it a feeling of well-being and lightheartedness.

There is no end to the number of possibilities available to mankind and that means each one of us. No end to the achievements we can accomplish, if only we would change our view of the world and our place in it.

Our achievements on the technological side have been somewhat revolutionary, but unless we open our minds to greater possibilities in the way we think, act and view our world, the imbalance between the two could well be our downfall.

What lessons have not been learnt tend to repeat themselves in history and in everything we do, until the lesson has been learnt. Not only acknowledging the lesson but actually learning from the lesson and using the wisdom that has been gained.

How many times has history repeated itself both in famines, wars and conflicts of every kind? We are here as a whole, not individual, not detached from each other but a whole. Together on a planet that needs our help and needs us to cooperate with each other, not in conflict with each other, and not between countries either. Nothing is ours, in fact, nothing belongs to anyone it is all on loan, it is all there for our use and our enjoyment. Also something to cherish and to care for, for the time that we are here, as we do not take any of it with us, only the lessons we have learnt from this life time and the growth we have made within that learning.

A tolerance now is needed and an acceptance of our differences, whether it be about colour, race or religion, a celebration of life for who and what we are. A wonderful mix of unique colourful individuals, all having our own paths, our own journeys in life, and all having our lessons to learn. All unique in every sense, just as everything is in the entire universe, each with its own identity shape and structure, all fitting in beautifully with the greater scheme of things.

Whereas every thought and action creates your reality, so to does every thought and action steer the direction of your life. Even in the smallest of ways, as you are the creator of your own destiny. Yes, the opportunity to be all you wish to be, how amazing is that!

Once you have realised this and indeed come to terms with the implications of such a discovery, then there are a great many options, and directions open to you. To too many people a very scary thought, as it means that you need to take responsibility for your life, it means you have to make decisions, it means you have to make a choice. As Nelson Mandela once said, "Our deepest fear is not that we are inadequate. Our deepest fear is that we are powerful beyond measure. It is our light, not our darkness, that most frightens us. We ask ourselves, who am I to be brilliant, gorgeous, talented and fabulous?

Actually, who are you not to be?

It is to this end, that we need to take action not only for ourselves, but also in our home and in our workplace. In fact at every level in our lives, even to the upbringing of our children, from every avenue of our existence. To leave no stone unturned until we are at peace, until we are content, until we are totally happy with who and what we are being in our life's experience here on earth.

A time of contemplation and a time of searching deep within our souls to bring our lives and spirits back in line to what we chose to do and be, a time of realignment and adjustment at all levels of our entirety. Every action has a reaction here on earth, it has a reaction on our spiritual being too. For we are spirit, we are light, our short experience here on earth is purely a blip in our existence as a spirit, and spirit is truly what we are.

There is no other way to say this, we are spirit, whether it is acknowledged or not, in this lifetime's experience.

Once people come to realise this, and implement it in their everyday lives, then they have the ability to change anything that they feel is not working for them, or what they feel is inappropriate to what they wish to experience.

You know from your own feelings, what works for you and what doesn't? It is a feeling that comes from the heart and not the head, a feeling, knowing it is right, instead a feeling of dread and do I really have to do this?

The answer is no, you do not. It is only your preconceived ideas about who you are and what life you believe is mapped out for you. Your true potential being blocked by the, "I ought to" or the "I should do!" There is no such thing, only in your own mind. It is not selfish to do or be as you wish to do or be, as it is the whole point about your journey and experiences here, they have nothing to do with anyone else.

A question of what is right for you and what works in your world and what doesn't. That does not mean that you throw caution to the wind and go off in a tangent. It means taking time to contemplate where you are in the terms of your life's journey and whether what you are doing, and indeed what you are being fits and feels comfortable within the realms of who you are and who you wish to be. A matter of searching, yes, a searching within to find and feel what truly resonates with you in every aspect of your life. A tuning into the spirit that is you, and is there to guide you along your chosen path when given the opportunity, to do so.

It is only the constant doing that disables the communication between you, whether it be in a physical sense or constantly thinking of the next thing you have to do. The next thing you need to do and not have to do will come automatically, when given the chance through relaxation. That is why I believe the most powerful tool available to man is meditation. A time of stilling the mind and letting the communication between the physical body and the spirit that you are, communicate in a totally loving and constructive way.

Opening up the channel of communication between you, in a way that is most beneficial to you both, in the human and spiritual form.

The mere mention of meditation to some people, throws up all sorts of visions, sitting crossed legged on a floor with hands in their knees or chanting some kind of dirge. Yes, some people do, and they choose to do this, because it resonates with them and feels right for them to do it this way, but there really is no need, and it certainly is not required.

All that is needed is a quiet moment to yourself, a comfortable place to sit and relax and be at peace with where you are. To close your eyes, and as much as possible withdraw yourself for a while from all that is around you and all that is going on in your world.

When thoughts come to you of what you think you should be doing instead, let them pass, it is only your brain doing what it has always done, it is only natural, with a little time and patience it will learn to quieten.

It will depend a great deal on the amount of time you give yourself for relaxation generally and how much stress you feel in the course of your day. It varies from person to person, but there is no one who will not benefit, and no one that it is unsuitable for. Relaxation is the most undervalued and under rated past time in our world today.

Not only is it highly beneficial to have such moments of relaxation, but also to have time amongst nature. Go into the countryside or the nearest park or gardens, as these are great sources of energy, both to our body and to our soul. A drawing in of natural energy, to be at one with nature, a natural healer, and a good way to rebalance.

It has also been said that time is a great healer, but I personally have not always found this to be true, but to be at one with nature or at least be surrounded by it, is the greatest healer that I know. Not only this, but it also gives you a sense of well-being, and helps you in your everyday activities.

Why? Because it is natural and one of the areas on this planet that is closest in relation to who we are. It grows, is a living organism, takes in sustenance and has intelligence just like our selves albeit in a different form.

This is why whenever we go out and be amongst nature, we have a sense of calmness and peace. At least that is, if we are open to its qualities and its abilities, and take the time to feel its effect. Time to feel its gentleness and marvel in all that it gives us, for without it life on this planet could not be sustained.

A blending of energies, for everything is energy, and to blend with something that is so pure and natural can only benefit those who do.

It is just a question of a deeper understanding of who and what you really are, and understanding to that you are part of nature, just as it is part of you. To blend with something that is part of who you are, is connecting in part to your self and being in touch with your senses, which will give you a greater connection to who and what you really are. A spirit, a timeless spirit, of countless gifts and talents all there for your choosing, so what is it that you would like to do and be?

Of course, it isn't just that simple, first you need a dream, ultimately, your goal and focus. Something to shape your direction, something you have always wanted to do or be, no matter how far-fetched, or unattainable it seems to be. For as with all things they need to be nurtured, and they need to be fed for them to flourish and grow, a planting of a seed and encouraging it as you would a small child.

To have a dream is to have your focus in life and is connected to your life experiences and what you came here ultimately, to do and be and why you chose to be here at this time. Everyone has a dream or did at some point in their lives. Whether it is attainable or not is entirely dependent upon their focus and effort to bring these dreams to fruition.

Dreams are very powerful, and given the chance can lead you in a totally different direction from one that you are now experiencing. Just because you are leading one particular kind of life, does not mean it has to stay this way, or that there is nothing you can do to change it, if you so desire at any age. It is mainly a question of applying yourself to that possibility and a belief in yourself which really counts, along with the courage and determination to make the necessary changes needed to bring your dreams into the realm of reality.

Living the life you are now, but also directing your life in the direction of your dreams, taking every opportunity open to you to steer you along this desired path and ultimately to your path in life. I cannot say what these directions are as everyone's dream is unique to themselves, and every dream unique to the person in question. You will know from your own heart, which form they need to take. It may be something as simple as taking a course in a particular subject, it may be a totally change of lifestyles and direction to get you to where you desire to be. In any event, whatever draws you closer to that dream can only be a step closer to that reality.

It depends very much on your position now in life and how far along that path you already are. It will depend to on your age and your dreams becoming a reality, although I did hear of a lady learning to fly a plane and getting a pilot's license at 75 years of age and a neighbour of mine in her 90s learning Italian and loving it! So do not let age limit you in your possibilities, and what you think is open to you and what is not, as the possibilities are endless.

To live life's dream is what I feel life's journey is really all about.

To Dream Life's Dreams

Oh tiny baby gazing out at this wondrous world

What do you think and what do you see?

Who knows the wonders yet to unfold?

So many things that make you giggle with glee

Surrounded by boundless beauty to behold

How you will long to be free

Free as a bird journeying to places untold

Dream on, as all too soon it will be

The time where you are told

That to have such aimless fantasy

Is only for those who refuse to grow old

A never ending adventure from our birth here to our departure onto pastures new, from whence we came. A journey of discovery and joy, and yes the hard times too of which I have experienced many, but have all lead to a greater understanding of life and a growth of which I could never have achieved in any other way, both spiritually and physically.

There was never a better time in all of man's history, than now to use the energies that are available, to evolve and to grow into all you have ever wanted or dreamed you could be. The energies around at this time are so immense, so powerful that anything is possible and indeed conceivable if you believe it to be so.

A question of belief in yourself and what you intend to do and be in this world and ultimately be as a spirit. Not one of looking at others and seeing what they are achieving and doing, but one of a focus on oneself and the courage and determination to bring your ideas and dreams into being, into the realm of materiality, instead of them just being ideas and thoughts.

There are many avenues to be explored, and each of us needs to take a more responsible role, for the choices we make now will determine the outcome, not only of the lives we live, but also to the planet and future life on this planet to.

DIFFERENCES

Where there are opposites of anything in this world and there are many, there will always be conflicts off some kind you would say but why?

Living in a world of such diversity, of different cultures, religions, colour and creeds is wonderful. A world full of differences to enrich and delight both our minds and our senses.

To be in a world where everything was the same would be like eating the same meal every day or repeating the same things over and over again. Not such a wonderful idea!

Differences are for embracing and delighting in, to respect and to behold, to cherish and to wonder at. Such diversity, such an amazing ray of colour, thoughts and ideas, each of us with our own true identities, each with our own tale to tell, each with our own talents and gifts of every kind. A whole world of cultural differences to be cherished and be seen as a huge advantage that it is, so much to learn from each other and so much to give each other to, in many ways.

You see, in this world, where there are so many cultural differences, it's not just a case of accepting those differences, but one of learning. Learning from each culture and embracing what each country and culture has to give in ways that will benefit all of us and all of mankind. For each of us in our own way has something to give, whether it be in a huge dramatic way or something more subtle, but nonetheless just as important. As with each of these things whatever they may be are a part, an important part of the whole.

We all have an important role to play, each of us in our own way, no one is more important than the next, no one has a greater standing than the next, we are all equal, we are all spirits.

In any event, past or present it is the moment that we are in now that counts, as anything that has past and gone is purely memory and not to be associated with what is in this present moment and which is relevant to the now.

That does not mean to say that anything that is or has gone before is irrelevant, as everything is for consciousness and everything has a purpose and a place in our memory and our moments. It is a case of learning from each moment and learning from what has gone before and not repeating past mistakes or shall I say learning opportunities.

Everything that we experience in our lifetime here has a purpose and a place in our consciousness, something that is acknowledged, learnt from or used and then hopefully moved on from. I say, hopefully as it all depends on the learning experience and whether or not we have taken on board the experience that was intended for our growth and development. If this lesson is ignored or not taken on board it is repeated, sometimes over many lifetimes, until the said lesson or experience has been learnt. Not only learnt and acknowledged, but used to its full extent. A lesson or learning experience is never fully learnt until is used and used in the manner it was intended. Sometimes, only part of a lesson has been learnt or used and in these cases the lesson will be repeated in a different form or format.

These learning curves and experiences are circles that each of us participate in, knowingly or unknowingly, and these circles are experiences that repeat themselves in many different forms until the lesson has been learnt. The circle grows, we expand both in our knowledge and in our understanding, our experiences become more colourful and meaningful as we expand that circle, we increase in our knowledge and wisdom of life, our intended journey and path become more clear to us.

So as we journey through many lifetimes, it is these experiences and learning that we take with us to enrich our souls knowledge and wisdom. A growth that can only come from living through what was intended and taking from it the jewel or gift that the said experience was. For every experience has a gift for you of different kinds, some you may not welcome or at the time be in total despair over, but they are all gifts of one kind or another, all intended to move you on to a higher plane of understanding. A better understanding of yourself, life, and also of the universe of which you are part.

To have a better understanding of yourself is to have a better understanding of others also, for without this understanding there can be no concept of what life is truly about or what another soul is experiencing or going through. It is an understanding of who you truly are, in terms of your journey and reason for being here at this time, for everyone is in the right place at the right time, and everyone has a reason and purpose for being here, whether it is acknowledged or not.

Some souls change their minds and go. A spirit has the freewill to go, if it so chooses. Call it a reset button if you like, a change of course, a change of direction due to many thousands of reasons of various kinds. That is why there is no set age for us to depart this earthly plane, but one of a choice from our spiritual state, one that oversees all we think say or do. I will call it, our higher self where our guidance and past experiences, originate from. A higher self that knows us intimately and knows all our weaknesses and strengths, our past endeavours and past experiences of every kind.

There will have been times when you have been frightened of something for no good reason known to you. You have no idea in this earthly state, what has gone before or what triggered this feeling of fear you had, for whatever reason.

These things you do not need to know as knowing them would only hamper your experiences of your journey and lifetime here in this present existence. A past memory, a past experience, which has triggered this fear and if faced and dealt with in this lifetime, will not only help you overcome the fear in this lifetime but for all eternity.

So you see, it is a colourful journey with many facets and many opportunities for growth and learning of all kinds, regardless of age, colour or creed. As we are all the same, spirits ever evolving, ever growing in an ever expanding circle of life, one that we are all a part of and always will be. A small but important part of the whole, each on our own journeys, each with our own gifts and talents, each having a part to play in the grander scheme of things in our own way.

Some choosing to be all they can be, and deciding to make a stamp on the world. Others choosing a more, less adventurous path. Nonetheless, just as important, for you never know what a spirit has chosen to learn in this lifetime or what lessons are needed to be learnt for that spirit, to evolve, grow and to move on from.

A case of not judging what others are doing, being or thinking, but one of self-observation, self-understanding and self-growth, for understanding oneself is to be aware of who and what you really are.

Nonetheless, it is evident in many walks of life not only in this continent but all continents of the world, that many aspects of the self are hidden behind many agendas and past experiences, making it difficult to realise sometimes what is real and what is not. What is of consequence and what is not.

A never ending change of perspectives and viewpoints, depending on how you view your world and the experiences you have had to date. All stored in memory for use at another time, whether it be to remind you of something that has ended or to remind you of an unpleasant experience, not wanting to repeat. In fact data of all kinds from the experiences you have had.

Everyone's experiences will be different and relevant to who they are and their journey through life, so therefore everyone's perspective and viewpoints will be different too, each one, having a different experience to the next person, each having a different outcome and therefore a different perspective and viewpoint of the same situation.

It is these experiences in different forms that make journeys so unique to each one of us, and it is for us to embrace that uniqueness both in ourselves and other people. To know and embrace that in others too, accept that each of us is different. Accept that each of us is unique and know that each of us will always view a very similar situation differently through our own view and experience of the same similar situation and to be mindful of this at all times in the dealings with others. Having an open mind to all possibilities and other people's experiences of the same, seemingly situation.

All too easy to judge another's actions, but without knowing the given situation or indeed knowing what the experience was like, is not to give another permission to feel worthy for their experience as they viewed it and experienced it.

It is of paramount importance in this stage of our involvement to be aware of others needs as well as our own on a daily basis, to take in account other's feelings and needs, and not purely our own.

We live in a society now, where generally little care is taken on what others feel; whether they are cared for or indeed loved. A society now in most cases built on greed and care not attitude for others or towards others in many capacities. It is a sad, but all too real a reality, where often people do not even acknowledge each other or have the time for any pleasantries in life any more. One of rushing from place to place, trying to cram in as much as possible but to what ends? What does it all achieve? A better way of living, a more purposeful life or a sense of satisfaction?

Well, from most of the gloomy looks from people I see around the world, none of these things are being achieved. In fact, I would say the opposite in many cases. An increasingly spiral of dissatisfaction and an increasingly dissatisfaction of life, and their place within it.

For all the gadgetry and modern conveniences to make our lives seemingly easier and less stressful, I do not see it having the desired effect, in fact I feel the contrary is happening.

Instead of enjoying the easier lifestyle, these wonderful technologies could bring us, we fill every moment of the day with something else. Seemingly not wanting to stop or relax in any way that nature and their journey was intended.

Life was never meant to be a constant treadmill, one of constant demands or deadlines, one of constantly being on the go, battling to get the next thing done. It's all about balance.

You have your own journeys, experiences and lessons to learn along the way.

I will call it our path in life, a path that is only trodden by you, unique to you in every sense. One that was devised by you, chosen by you, and one that takes you further along the path of your learning and your evolvement in this vast and wonderful universe of ours.

A journey not to be afraid of or thought of as selfish, by doing what feels right for you, but one of expansion and growth of the soul that you are. A wonderful soul of many facets, one that is longing to move forward in many ways. Which is not always the case in many souls journeys here on this earthly plane. Some have purely come to learn lessons from previous lifetime's, which sometimes need to be repeated and repeated until the said lesson is learnt. This may not take one lifetime but sometimes many, depending on the lesson and the progress of the spirit itself.

So you see journeys here are not clear-cut or defined, as we are all unique beings and each experience and lesson being unique to the souls journey and its stage of evolvement.

Whether it be a young spirit of little experience or wisdom, or a spirit that has evolved through many lifetimes and experiences has learnt and taken on board the learning intended, and moved on to higher planes.

Sometimes a spirit decides not to move forward, but to remain where it is, and feels more comfortable with what it knows and what it is experiencing. Very similar to our lifetimes experiences here. Some people like to remain in their known environment, with the things that they are comfortable with, not wanting to venture forth and explore the unknown. Eventually though all spirits move forward, as does the universe and everything in the universe. A wonderful breathing living organism designed and made for growth on all levels. Whether it be here on this planet, or a far distant galaxy, for there are many galaxies to be explored and the spirit will go to where ever the conditions are appropriate for the experience and lessons to be learnt. Not always in human form, but in a form that is relevant to the journey chosen for that particular experience.

An amazing concept of ingenuity and design, something we can only imagine but not even start to comprehend in our present form, I am meaning generally. That is to say, there have been many prophets and people in this world who have this foresight and wisdom of knowing another and several other existences other than the one we see around us.

Many who have tried to show the way, but in many cases been seen as scaremongers, when in fact what they have to offer and tell us in many cases is the truth.

There will always be the charlatans amongst us, who see themselves as better or above anyone else, and this will always be the case, as there are varying degrees of everything, from black to white, from rich to poor, from hot to cold, and from fact to fiction. It is for each of us to open our hearts and minds and decide what feels right for us, and what doesn't. Not to put people upon any pedestal and treat them as God's, as we are all God's in our own way, it is purely our journey and life's experiences and lessons in life that are different. We have no way of knowing their lessons or life's path, only the façade we see before us.

Each of us is spirit and spirit only, nothing less and nothing more, each one of us being part of the whole, none of us is no more special than the next, only in our minds eye, which is all it is! To put or see another as more worthy than yourself is to deny self-worth and your importance in the whole scheme of things, to undervalue your importance in this world and your place in it.

There are those who would have you think otherwise, but that would only be to further their own importance, a futile cause, for we are all spirit with no greater standing than the next. It is only here in our human form do some of us feel inferior or inadequate to perhaps some people who you would feel have a greater standing or position of importance on this mortal coil. But I tell you this; there is no difference between us only the parts we are playing, and only the façade that we portray to the world around us. Each playing various roles, each wearing our own disguises of various forms, relevant to the parts we are playing and relevant to lessons and experiences chosen, in our spiritual state.

So think not about what others are doing or being, the focus is on you and what you are doing and being, for it is your journey, your life's path that is important. It is for you to be all you can be in this world and to open your minds and hearts to a different life, if that is what you truly desire.

To want or dream about being another is only to shun who you really are, and to belittle the importance of who and what you really are - for we are all, Power, Grace and Beauty if we so decide to be. To be comfortable in our own skins, to be accepting of who and what we are. To see the beauty of all that is around us and to see each one of us as beautiful in our own unique way. As we are all made in God's own image, beautiful and perfect in our own ways. Each of us having all we need, both in looks and conditions for the life's experiences chosen in the spiritual state.

A concept some people may feel I expect, unbelievable, but in the life of a human spirit, we have no way of knowing their life's journey or in fact what has gone before, or what lessons this time have been chosen to learn.

Some people you see as being rich in this life may be totally poor in the next. The life of the spirit is complex and has many different facets to it, from age to experience, from expansion, to denial of self. It is all there in various forms being lived and played out in the reality of this world and the next.

So I have to smile sometimes when I'm told this person or that person has been here or there, or hold such people in such high esteem. They get totally absorbed in their lives, instead of a focus on their own and all they could do or be. A fascination that takes them away from their own life's journey, their learning and all they came here to be, in many cases.

Occasionally it is good to hold someone or some people in high esteem. One that can sometimes resonate with you and take you on to higher and greater expectations of yourself.

Also the case of spirits taking on a certain role in this lifetime, to bring about change or to be a role model in whatever form, to show people a different way forward, Some coming to set an example to others and some that put themselves on a pedestal purposefully, to show others how, not to be!

The wondrous combination of lives, circumstances and situations all playing out their own wonderful parts, in their own different ways.

There may be many times in people's lives when aspiring to another's achievements is very useful, it gives us incentive to do better, either in our appearance or in our own achievements and goals. Striving perhaps for a better quality of life, or it can give us a direction in one way or another that we had not thought of before. As with everything it is a case of balance and using others ideas or achievements in a way to enhance our own lives, but not to change it so radically that we lose sight of who and what we are about or what we are trying overall to achieve.

Success in life comes in many forms; it may not be just personal to you, it could be a team effort, something that is achieved through working with other people, some common goal or ambition. Whatever form it takes, it is always to be mindful of self, for self is who you are and it is your expansion, your evolvement that will determine your spiritual growth and overall journey as a spirit. For everything that is learnt and used in its entirety, will be learnt for all eternity and never to be repeated.

Anything not learnt and used will be repeated and repeated in a different form sometimes, until the lesson is learnt.

Have you ever noticed in your life how some things seem to come around and around?

It's difficult to set an example, as each has its own merit and is personal to you, but have you ever thought, "Why does so and so keep happening to me?"

Well that is a small example of what I mean. It could be something you keep saying or doing, it could be a malfunction with something you are using even (to direct you to using a different method). It could be something like always being late, to teach you to leave more time and to be more organised. It could be anything, but if you are mindful and make a conscious note of these things, they will soon become apparent to you, and when this happens you will be able to take conscious measures to rectify them and learn the lesson that was intended.

Some lessons are more difficult and some people are not even aware of their existence in their lives. The most common one that I have come across is in some marriages. A person or persons will have difficulties in his or her marriage and finally get divorced. Then marry again at some point and find they have the same difficulties as before but not even realising that this is the case at all. Not only in marriages but in relationships and how we relate to each other in business transactions and many other dealings in everyday life, sometimes completely unaware of the pattern emerging or the repeat of certain factors that have gone before.

It is a fascinating concept and once realised can be of great benefit to you in your life's journey. As I said, it's not just a case of saying, "I have learnt the lesson", but once learnt is used and used in all its entirety. A bit like a promise and the saying, "A promise is not a promise until it is delivered", and very apt in these instances.

It is to be conscious and mindful of what your life is truly about, to explore the reasoning behind your actions and to be mindful of your choices and the outcome of those choices, whether they serve you and your purpose or whether they do not. Whether they were beneficial to you or they were not, whether any lessons were learnt along the way or whether they were ignored and stored away, only to be repeated at a later date.

Only you and you alone know the answers.

TIME TO CHANGE

Wouldn't it be wonderful if a world existed that had no wars or famine, where everyone was honest and truthful to each other and worked side-by-side in any way that they could. Helping each other out, not just when there was a catastrophe but on a day to day basis.

A shift away from the negativity and the doom and gloom merchants, to the positivity of all that is wonderful and indeed magnificent in this world. Away from the greed of people and even more so of companies for ever thinking of their profit margins, to being more responsible for all concerned. Whether it be to their workers, their shareholders and more importantly to the land and ultimately the planet itself.

Workers taking a stand for a better more relaxing way of working and ultimately a more relaxed lifestyle, for stress and increased hours only stunts creativity and productive output. Longer hours and working weekends to get things done, only undermines the family structure, causes stress on all sides and a huge increase in sickness and stress-related illnesses.

We all need to think where our priorities lie and ultimately which direction we would like them to be heading. A choice from the heart, not one from the mind, a conscious choice, one that leads us away from the doom and gloom and out into a more positive, uplifting experience of life.

It is totally in our hands, each one of us to make a difference in everything we think say and do. To make each one of us proud of our achievements and proud of what we are doing and being, whether it be at home, in the workplace or out on the streets. It matters not for everything counts, every action every thought even has a reaction.

Negativity breeds negativity, positivity brings positive results and a feeling of well-being at every level. It takes nothing more than seeing the good in everything or the positive side to any given situation.

Everything is energy, cells and atoms resonating at very high levels normally but in the case of this planet at the moment, much lower than is necessary for it to be sustained over a long period of time. The energies of the people need to rise to bring about a more balanced planet and therefore a more sustainable one, for each of us to be more positive, brighter and lighter, which raises the energies of the planet too.

There comes a time in everyone's life when changes are needed to bring everything back in line and everything back in focus and into balance. It could take just one radical change or many changes of direction along life's rich pattern, one of deliberate and conscious action and hopefully, one of change for the better.

It needs thought, a focus on what you would like to change and ultimately what you would like the ultimate goal to be. A bit like making a cake, making sure all the ingredients are correct, preparing the cases, then mixing it and baking it to perfection with tender loving care.

Each one of us whatever position we hold on this mortal coil, from politician to government officials, from people in the public eye, to office workers and shop assistants. All of us across the board, need to make a difference, regardless of class colour or creed. Each one of us is important, each of us playing out our roles, each one of us just as important as the next. All supposedly working together.......... hmmm.

Unfortunately that's not what I see and find, it is very sad indeed, that most people are so insular not wanting to get involved shall we say, with anyone that they do not know or do not recognise. Trusting only those in their immediate surroundings, thinking that anyone outside of this, is immediately wanting something or trying to take something away from them, always in fear of letting their friendship and love go further than their own immediate loved ones or friends.

Okay, in some cases there are people who are out there to con you and to take from you, but on the whole the majority of people are above that kind of behaviour, and those that do not have a lot of learning to do.

This is not always the case of course, there is so much good and good being done in the world that so many never get to hear of it, as it seems only doom and gloom is mostly regarded as news. To hear more of the good and the good news, would have so much more of a positive outlook and help people to see more of the good, instead of the negativity and focusing so much on the gloom, that is portrayed.

Negativity, breeds negativity, "For as you sow, yeah shall reap",

So very true.

A much-needed swing to the positive is now required in both our outlooks and the way we are generally. It is not impossible, otherwise

I would not be writing this, but it is now of the utmost urgency in all corners of the globe and in all areas of our lives.

There is much being done by many groups and organisations to try and bring many issues of importance to those in position of power, but it is not for us to be complacent and think that there is nothing we can do for ourselves. If each of us changes in even small ways collectively, it makes the world of difference to each and every one of us.

Alas, there are many instances where nothing changes, even when people are given the opportunities to do so. These opportunities are often shunned and seen to be too difficult a task or something that is attainable to somebody else but not themselves, afraid that it may rock the boat in terms of the family or not wanting to make the effort to bring about change in a direction that would bring benefits to all concerned, in the long run.

There are no such things as coincidences, just opportunities that are given to us at a moment in time that is relevant to you. Purely gifts in the form of opportunities which could be in various disguises, but all there for us to grasp and use, if we so choose.

It is in the choices that we make, that determines our destiny or future life and lives. It is in that choosing, do you decide who and what you wish to be, period. No set pattern or pre-ordained destiny, just choices made by you and no one else, both in the human and spiritual state.

There are always exceptions to the rule, for as I said earlier those people who come to truly help will know and follow their path to the letter normally. They will know this deep down and be totally focused on what they came here to do and be, but even then they have a choice, all spirits have a choice.

Total love and free will is for everyone.

Many people will dispute the fact that our destiny is what we choose it to be, as this would mean making changes, making an effort and doing something sometimes out of the ordinary. That is absolutely fine, as I say, it is all about making choices and the choices you make determine your future both on this planet and in your future lives.

An opportunity or gift passed by is a golden opportunity missed indeed, they are not gone for good but may or may not repeat themselves in your lifetime. It so depends on the timing and whether you are ready to embrace such changes again.

Your advancement as a spirit and the evolution of your soul depends so much on the willingness to embrace change. The whole universe is about change and changes constantly and you being a part of the whole, needs to change at some time or another. Eventually you will as all spirits do, the time taken to do so is all down to you and when you are ready and willing to do so.

An amazing circle of lives, opportunities and coincidences, all perfectly timed and designed for you and the choices you made prior to your life's experience here. In timely fashion for your advancement and what you have chosen to do. A never-ending adventure called life.

So many wonderful books have been written on the subject of life and the thereafter, but life is a continuation of 'what is' whether the life of the soul is having a human experience or not. It is all part of the same life cycle, all part of the universe as a whole and all part of who you really are.

A wonderful mix of energy so magical, so intricate in design and so complex that it is impossible to comprehend such complexities in our present human state, and that is the wonderful way it is meant to be. If we could even start to comprehend the workings of the universe and our lives of a spirit, our natural state. Somehow we would, or some people would want to try and control or try to change things, when indeed they are perfect both in design and their amazing capacity to be all they are meant to be.

It is only our human mind that thinks any different, thinking that something is wrong, something needs changing. Which is all an illusion for we have all we need within us and around us for all our needs, if only we could come to terms with that.

Everything is perfect – well was – until we decided we were smarter and far cleverer than the universe itself. Everything is and was provided, in perfect balance for all our needs. Even the technology is perfect in its own way, but just as with everything, needs to be used in a loving and positive way. In a way that benefits all, in a positive and healthy manner and was never intended to be used in a negative way - in destruction.

In fact nothing was ever intended to be used in a negative fashion, all was intended to benefit man, but as with everything we have a choice, free will to do as we please, a love that transcends all others.

It is no good us saying why does God let this happen and that happen, why doesn't God stop it. You cannot have free will one moment and not the next; it is for us to choose how to live our lives. We have been given the wonderful gift of life and it is for us to embrace it and love it, to see the magic in it and all it is and can be.

A magical journey of adventure it can be or a journey of doom and gloom and destruction.

What is it you choose?

For what you choose now and at any time denotes the very future and structure of the world we live in. Each one of our choices is important as collectively they make up the whole, and what each one of us does, says or thinks, causes a chain reaction and not only affects you but all around you. A chain reaction, a reaction to your action of minor or major magnitude depending on the action but a reaction just same and causes many other factors to come into play.

For as tiny seeds an Acorn tree grows, which will either flourish and bear fruit or wither and die, depending on the conditions around it and what it is dependent on.

Like a child who has to be nourished, loved and cared for; for it to grow into a strong human being, full of health and vitality if it is cared for in the appropriate loving way. The same is for the planet and for ourselves, each needing that same tender loving care.

It is for us to do that for ourselves once we have grown and are able to do so and for us to look after those who are unable, like children. The disabled and the planet that looks to us to care for it in a loving and caring manner, for we are the caretakers and guardians of planet Earth.

APPRECIATION

Look around you what you see, a plant, a tree perhaps, hopefully something natural and living, giving you pleasure on the mere sight of it.

There is beauty all around us, in many forms and in many shapes and sizes, a bit like us really all different and unique in our own way. We all need nourishment, we all need light and space to live and breathe. We all have our own ways of taking in moisture and nourishment, and a way of discarding what we no longer need. The trees will take their nourishment from the soil and from the environment around them, and we take it from food we eat, which is mainly grown in the soil and gets its nourishment from the same source.

We breathe in the air just the same; the only difference is that the tree is designed to draw in from the air which we no longer need in the form of carbon dioxide. A beautifully designed system of keeping the air healthy for us to use, for without it we could not survive.

The perfect conditions are provided not only for us but for all other living things. Be it for plants, animals, insects, in fact everything that is alive. So we have not only a responsibility to ourselves but to all living things that look to us for life and the conditions that they can thrive in.

Have you ever wondered or thought about the intelligence that trees and plants have? How they drop their seeds or get picked up on the wind and get blown to a different location, and will settle there until such a time that the conditions are perfect for their germination and growth. How each flower knows when it is time to flower, when to open and when to close.

So doesn't it make you wonder, how all this is possible and how it came to be?

I know I do but can only hazard a guess and that is all it will ever be, as to have that kind of knowledge would mean having some kind of control, and as yet we cannot even manage our own affairs on this planet never alone considering others out there in the galaxy!

We have everything we need on this planet for survival and for a wonderful way of living and being, it is for us to find the ways in keeping with nature and the planet to bring this about. There is nothing out there in space that we need or can help us; it is here around us and indeed within us, all the knowledge and the learning of millions of people with which to work with and use. A coming together of similar minds and wisdom that has been passed down the ages and for some reason if it has been a natural solution, being disregarded as irrelevant not able to work because it is indeed natural.

It is this working with nature and using it to its full potential that will bring the many changes needed to bring this planet back to an even keel. One of balance, and one of harmony, treating the cause at every level, and not just the symptoms as so often happens. Being responsible for ourselves instead of thinking it is purely down to others, and above all having the belief and courage to do something about it.

It needs countries coming together and realising that we are all one and all on this planet together and what one does affects each one of us in different ways.

It needs a realisation that we have all we need on this planet and to use the resources we have in a beneficial and responsible way. To realise that we are a tiny planet amongst millions of others and that is only in this galaxy. To open our minds and hearts to a greater existence, for to think this is all there is, is to be blinkered and small in the greater scheme of things.

I am no scientist or biologist for that matter but realise there must be a better way of fuelling cars, heating our homes, and providing power. There is immense power of the seas, the wind and even power not seen under the surface of the planet, just waiting to be tapped into and only felt when there is an eruption for the forces stored there have no other outlet, and nowhere else to go except upwards.

There is great power in the plants around us that have been used in treating ailments since time began but of course do not make profits like artificial drugs do.

Then there is the power of the mind, something so powerful and so wonderful and yet so under estimated and undervalued. It can bring so many changes both to our lives, our health and well-being, and the way we think and see ourselves - in a totally different light.

So all these things I feel have not been explored enough in positive and new ways. Some avenues have been explored, but quite often it's a case of cost effectiveness and yet we spend billions in other areas in a negative and destructive manner.

It is time now to look back in history and see what has worked, what has not, and what is beneficial to us now and what is best left where it is, in the past. A memory sometimes a painful one but memory just the same. A time to move on from where we are today and where we wish to be tomorrow, for there is only the here and now, tomorrow will be our today but yesterday is gone and past. We can only hopefully learn from our experiences of the past, for that is the whole point of an experience, to learn and decide not to repeat past mistakes and move on to a better brighter future.

Yes in many areas there is a need for improvement both in our attitude and responsibility to both ourselves, and this wonderful planet Earth. It needs countries, governments, companies and indeed all of us to make a concerted effort to bring much needed changes about. A feat which is not impossible by any means but one that needs focus of vision, determination and courage to make the changes so desperately needed at this time.

A coming together now of great minds is needed, regardless of race or religion, bringing all their talents and expertise together to find solutions, natural solutions to the problems facing us.

Enough, enough I hear you cry, it's all too much, it's all doom and gloom!

Well no, actually it's not, there are some great things happening. One or two countries already are seeing the need for change and vastly improving their methods of farming, waste and better ways to make power, I believe.

Whether you be rich or poor young or old, there is always room for change even in the smallest of ways, from having a good clear out from all that is no longer useful or have a place in your life, to a total change of life and lifestyle.

Anything that constitutes a positive change is a move forwards. Change for the sake of change is something quite different and just moves one focus to another without having actual benefits of any lasting kind. The difference between the first and the second is a sense of direction and purpose, whether it be just clearing out an over congested cupboard or thinking perhaps along the lines of a new career, both quite different, but each with its own sense of purpose.

The second is purely a move from one to the other, without any preconceived thought or focus, a lack of direction or purpose as to why you are doing it. This is lacking in definition with no particular target in mind. Not even a clean and tidy cupboard!

Some people have their focus and have known all their lives their direction they wish to take and who or what they wish to be. Others though, through the periods of their lives have not lost but forgotten their aim, forgotten their focus and their true lives focus and direction. Sometimes through circumstances of their lives and sometimes through a feeling of what they think they need to do or should do. In either case, it is to refocus that direction lost in whatever way you can.

You may need guidance, you may need just some time out to be alone and contemplate where you would really like the direction of your life to be heading. You may have given up on a long lost dream that you thought was impossible at that time and may find new ways of rekindling that dream you once had, now.

There is no time like the present; it is about making the best of the opportunities open to you. Opening up new doorways and avenues to explore, one appertaining to you and your life and not others, making sure they are your dreams and ambitions, your focus and your direction.

I say this, for only too often people, well meant people have a need somehow of telling others what they feel others should or should not be doing with their lives. A need to take the focus away from themselves - but that's another time.

It is not what others think you should or should not be doing but you yourself making up your own mind and your own direction.

As I say the life of the spirit is very varied and complex, no other person can make those decisions for you, that is for you to do. Others can help you find a direction though by giving you ideas or sometimes leads, an introduction perhaps to someone who knows someone, who is looking for a person just like you. A chance meeting of someone who triggers a past memory of something you wanted to do but thought had gone away.

They never go away, they are stored in your subconscious waiting for an appropriate time to re-emerge that's all. Waiting for the time of your reemergence of it to bring it back into being, back to where it belongs in the now - when you are ready for it to be.

As one door closes another one opens and true for us either in this human experience or in our spiritual state. We shut the door on what has been and open another to the new and awaiting experience.

A never ending chain of opportunities for us to expand and grow as a spirit, for that is the reason for being here. To learn, expand our knowledge of ourselves and the universe, in ways that are unique to us and from the perspective of being in a physical form and the experiences that come with being as such. It is a totally different experience, different from any other and experienced in the tangibility and the physical form with all the limitations that go with being as such.

As a spirit we are free to go wherever we please and not have the restraint of the body and all its functions. Inhibited and weighed down some would say by its awkwardness and somewhat basic capabilities, like having to eat food to nourish us, using cars and vehicles to get us around from place to place. Having to speak to communicate with one another and wearing clothes to keep us warm or covered in some way, depending on the climate of where we live.

All of these and more are alien to us in our natural state, for we are energy, pure energy that needs none of these things; a concept that many would find hard to believe.

That is why when we arrive - born onto this planet we now regard as home, we arrive with a blank sheet and everything we see, touch, smell and experience we think is all new to us and of course to some of us it is, depending whether you have ever been here previously and had similar experiences. To others their memory is still blanked out but some have experiences of déjà vu and a knowing of previous experiences here, having a better understanding of languages and sometimes lets say, know their way around certain things more easily.

Still regardless of this, we all come with gifts and talents of one kind or another, all equipped with what we need for this life's experience. Some come with gifts of being able to play music or paint or have other natural gifts that they bring with them to help them in this life's experience. We all come with different aptitudes to be all we came here to be. Some are apparent from a very early age, others are learnt through skills and training because that is what we chose to do, others come into being at a later stage in life, when we finally realise our true life's journey and purpose.

Some of us will find our true path by having a passion for something, you will know what it is and it is always something that you love and enjoy doing, cooking, gardening, sailing, decorating, the list is endless, as is all the opportunities for us to be all we wish to be in this lifetime.

Not to settle for something that stresses us, inhibits us, makes us groan on a Monday or whatever day!

One that uplifts us, gives joy to us, and makes us feel good about ourselves both in what we are doing and what we are being, both to ourselves, and all those we come into contact with.

For if we shine and love life as was always the intention, then it not only brims over and touches other people's lives with your joy and enthusiasm, but also shows others that they too can live a life of joy and contentment. Happy in the knowledge that they are doing and being all they can be.

A far cry I feel from what is taking place around us at this present time with a few exceptions of course, there are those that are happy and content with their lives. Happy in the knowledge that they are doing and being what they came here to be - for now.

I say for now, as life has a way of changing and you might not have come here to be and experience just one thing but many. In fact it is very rare for it to be just one or a few things. It depends so much on what you have come to learn, what you have come to do, how long all this takes to come about and whether or not you actually achieve your aims and goals in this lifetime.

It is very common for people to reach their later years and suddenly have the realisation that they have not achieved what they set out to do, not been to the places they wish they had, when they had the opportunity to do so or even said or settled things, like disputes with people. Instead they have stored up their issues letting them fester causing blockages within, which turn in some cases to bitterness, resentment and in many cases to illness and disease. These things need to be said and dealt with along the way, for without doing so have no escape, no outlet, nowhere to go except within and are very destructive not only to our own physical well-being but also to our spiritual being that we take with us when we go! Along with all the attitudes, misconceptions doubts and fears, all to be dealt with at a later date.

Having a clear conscience and peace of mind goes a long way to having good health and well being, both in the physical and spiritual.

Over the hills and far away, where the grass is always greener – so they say.

Well – sometimes, sometimes it is a change of location and country to bring about the change that is required in a certain situation. Something that you cannot achieve or want to achieve in your present place or location. In some cases though it is more of a running away from a certain factor or situation before it has been satisfactorily dealt with or had closure.

A running away - yes, instead of facing whatever it is that needs your attention and ultimately to be dealt with!

It could be anything, but the person in question will know only too well what it is and what they are trying to run away from.

There is NOTHING that can be LEFT UNDONE!

There is nothing that can be left undone, nothing that can be omitted or left behind. It is only in your mind that you think you are free of it; there is no escape from lessons to be learnt only from your perception of the situation!

SPIRITUAL GROWTH

Silence is our natural state of being and quite often it is the noise and distractions of this world that inhibit us from listening to our inner voice or our guidance that will enable us and to help us to find and achieve our directions more easily, in fact far more easily. Our inner voice knows all our inner secrets, our inner strengths and weaknesses, knows our journey our past experiences and our ultimate goals, whilst here on this planet, and most importantly what we came here to do and be.

We all have this inner voice, that is what is meant by going within, quieting the mind and connecting to your spirit, your soul who you really are.

Pausing a few minutes to collect your thoughts some would say, which is the same thing. It is this realisation of knowing that you are more than you see in the mirror, a realisation of something greater than what you see before you, opening up a whole new world of possibilities for you to explore, a depth that has no level, a source that has no limits or expectations from you or anything.

A place within where all is peaceful and calm, a sanctuary for all who wish to go there; albeit for a few moments contemplation or a longer period devoted to oneself, a period of reflection or to find one's direction and path in life. Sometimes being able to restore one's balance, to calm the mind and a place to see a different perspective on certain situations and life.

A place so serene, so gentle and so loving that on occasions I have not wanted to leave. Strange then that so many do not wish to go there or acknowledge its existence, for all of us go there from time to time either knowingly or not, in moments of quietness or solitude, moments of thought or ponderings. Moments when you lose yourself in thought and not exactly here in the present moment of time.

Ah you say, is that where I go? Yes exactly, a place within a place where only you can be, a special place that is you, the real you and not what you perceive yourself to be - well in most cases.

This is what is called 'going within' to the spirit that is you, the real you in your natural state. Where all your instincts come from, your hunches, your dreams and ambitions where all your life's path memory is stored and all that is known to you for your use and assistance in this life's journey. Without which you would have no data, guidance or any idea what so ever about who and what you are about or why you are taking this journey at all.

So very little thought is given to where all these ideas and such things come from for it certainly is not your brain; as your brain only stores up past or present knowledge to be used and recalled on when a certain situation repeats itself. You have the knowledge of the past experience to draw on whether it be to drive a car, swim, walk and words that you have learnt to speak in the country of your origin. This is all stored in the brain, just data and knowledge as in the computer, files downloaded as and when required, as long as you have not deemed them unnecessary any more and have forgotten!

Instincts and intuitions are totally different and come from 'yourself', from within at your core level; a prompting, a guiding hand to lead you along this life's path and journey, one that was chosen in your spiritual state, before your coming to be here. These guidance's and hunches are here to guide you along your chosen path and there may be times when some of you will look back on your life and see the opportunities and coincidences that happened along the way and see how they bought you to the moment that you are now experiencing.

You may look back and see how many opportunities were missed or for one reason or another you decided they were not for you or were too difficult a task, or it meant that you would have to move away or give up something that you were not willing to do. There are a host of reasons and many different situations unique to each person, but opportunities they are none the less, and it is for you to choose whether or not you wish to do them. Some are repeated further along your path if at that time you passed up on them but others are a one time opportunity that needed to be grabbed at the time or the moment and opportunity is gone forever at least within this lifetime anyway – never learnt or never experienced. Purely your choice and a case of free will for everyone.

Some of these opportunities come at a very early age, to some of us much later on in life, each on his or her own unique journey each on their own paths finding their way through the maze called life and making of it what they will with what they have and the opportunities that present themselves to them. Not everyone decides to have an adventurous life or even a fascinating one, for as I said earlier you have absolutely no idea of what that person came here to do or be, or indeed what is their intention and ultimately their reason for being here on this planet at this time. What lessons they came to learn or what their previous lives entailed.

A fascinating mishmash of spirits and souls each figuring out their best way through, each endeavouring to do the best with what they have and being all they can be – well that is the intention anyway. Far be it for me to say otherwise, but I really sometimes look around and wonder if this really is the case or whether people have forgotten what life is truly about and whether it is a free for all with no direction or real thought about life's purpose, their journey. Where they really came from, or asking the age-old question, which really should be forthright in most people's thoughts.

What is life all about?

Not one designed to be a chore or an uphill struggle all the time, not one of segregation, insular groups of people and certainly not one of constant wars, famine, selfishness and greed but one more based along the lines of caring and sharing in an appropriate way, one of thinking more about others but at the same time preserving our boundaries and sense of self-worth. An olive branch held to those in need, and compassion for those less fortunate than ourselves. Not a defining line, where everything is black and white but one of discernment and caring in a method appropriate to the cause in question. Whether it would ultimately help in a positive and productive way and also whether the purpose intended is leading them to their goals and ambitions of this lifetime.

Nothing is cut and dry, they all need to be looked at carefully for their merit and what it is that the person or persons concerned that need help with and are trying to achieve. For sometimes where we think we may be helping, maybe in fact not be helping in the long run at all, but only delaying the process of them coming to the realisation of life and what it is they need and in fact can do for themselves but compassion and kindness in any case, is a necessary part of the helping I believe.

A world without compassion and kindness would be a very sad place indeed.

It is always to look at the cause of a person's malaise and not always what is obvious from an onlookers viewpoint, to delve into what has gone before and what has brought them to the place they now find themselves. You cannot expect a person who has been brought up on violence from an early age not to know any other way but violence, unless another way has been shown to them or experienced.

Just as we grow up learning and soaking up all that is around us; it is so dependent on the conditions of our upbringing and what we experience along the way and is true in every case whether it be a loving close family or violent family where little or no love is experienced or shown.

So many instances, where teenagers are locked away with other people of the same upbringing or experiences never having the opportunity to experience or know of any other way. Again this is not always the case; there are never any hard and fast rules in anything ever. Some people get a great deal of help and often find their lives are turned around. Others decide that it is not for them and make the decision to be different, and not to change the way they are. Never getting the opportunity to move on and grow.

It can always be done in every case it's just a matter of choice, the willingness to change and be different from what they were. Not only in these instances but from our upbringings we can decide to walk and be like our families and our parents, or we can choose our own path. It depends so much on the love and support – the nourishment you have been given along the way – meaning the nourishment of the spirit and the mind, in ways of encouraging you on the path or career you have chosen and not chosen for you. You may have been steered in a direction that you love – which is wonderful and all part of your life's rich pattern and path in life, but if it is not for you then you will know from how you feel inside, your heart will tell you if indeed it feels right for you and if it resonates with you.

There are no ought to's or should do's in this world, it all has to be of your choosing, but choose wisely and carefully for this is not a dress rehearsal – as they say – it's the real thing.

So many times a parent has failed to achieve their aims and goals, then try and satisfy their own sense of failure through the eyes of their child. Thinking in most cases this is the best for their offspring, not realising that they are wanting to relive their dreams that they once had for their own lives. They push and drive their child or children into a path that is not of their own choosing and not a path that they were destined for. It is in these cases that a parent really needs to ask themselves the question. Am I pushing for my own gratification? Is this really what my child would love to do and be?

Just because a parent may frown upon a certain profession and think it not suitable, or would somehow feel embarrassed in some way for a child to follow a certain direction, does not mean it is inappropriate for the child. It may well be part of both their lessons in life; the child to pursue their chosen path regardless, or the parent to learn to love and support the child in whatever way is appropriate to the child and not themselves.

A fascinating world full of adventures, full of all sorts of possibilities to enable us to evolve and grow as a spirit. So many, many directions for us to choose and so many instances where we need to be brave and have the courage of our own convictions.

A stilling of the mind and a listening to the heart is all that is required, the heart being the voice within, the direction, our path, our focus and ultimate goals here on planet Earth.

MAKING A DIFFERENCE

So where do we go from here, upwards and onwards to a new glorious revival?

I do hope so; it would be such a waste to let such a wonderful beautiful planet go to ruin and waste. Not that the planet will not survive, it will.

I was thinking more about the human beings around that would have a hard time trying to live and cope in the world that had been left to its own devices and had not been looked after and loved. Not been given all it needs to remain balanced and stable.

A lesser desire of things that we do not need, so much of in the way of food for one thing, especially the amount of meat that is consumed in particular, the choices we make to nourish our bodies and the way we make choices about the way we live and move about on this planet.

So many of our choices are made in relation to cost instead of quality and what we are consuming and where indeed it came from and how it came to being into our lives. A desire for more responsibility not only to ourselves, our health and well-being but to the way it has been brought to tables to eat in the way of love and kindness on its life's journey to that table. For animals are no different from ourselves and need to be given the same respect and kindness that we would or should be giving to another.

The escalation of population and the escalation in the demand for meat has brought about the slaughtering of animals on a commercial basis, with no regard to the feelings of the animals or the way these demands are met, mostly. It is as though we see it as our right and animals are just there for our use and our carnivorous desires is ludicrous.

In the days of the caveman, when the only food available in the ways of protein was usually animal then it was a necessary action to survive. That was a long time ago and the universe and the planet have moved on in the ways of technology and commerce, but it seems man has not evolved in relation to this change or his desires, which are not necessary or healthy in the way it is either produced or the amount consumed – generally speaking and of the norm. It is the quantity that is demanded that is fuelling the problem and the greed to make heftier profits from such.

We bury our heads so much from all that is going on around us, not wanting and sometimes not even wanting to know the conditions of the animals being bred for slaughter, not wanting to know how chickens for instance got to such a bloated size or what chemicals went into making something a certain appealing colour.

THERE ARE MANY WHO DO CARE and take the trouble to rear their cattle and sheep well, give the animals is a good life and are ever thoughtful about what is used in the healthy and successful rearing of such animals. But so much more needs to be done in this direction. We the consumers can do so much to bring about this change in this now urgent situation. It is in your choosing and in your desires that will bring this much-needed change about, it's not down to the suppliers, for it is supply and demand and it is ourselves that are demanding such things!

It would all change so wonderfully and so would our unhealthy bodies if we made more discerning choices, one that is more in keeping with the natural composite of our bodies.

They were never designed for what we put into them now, they are natural and need natural foods to keep them healthy. Foods that have not been prepared days and even weeks ahead, taking away most or all of the nutrition that was intended in them for you. Neither is the amount of food consumed, necessary to keep us fit and healthy, there is an abundance of everything for everyone in this world if only we would learn to moderate our consumption and not see eating as a way of comforting ourselves and find the need to be nourished in other ways.

It is not to say, not to enjoy eating food, as it is a very pleasurable experience and one to be enjoyed but to look at why sometimes people overindulge and eat to excess, and this is an increasing problem around the globe.

Not to focus on dieting and other means of losing weight, but not putting the excess on in the first place and realise that there is a reason for this excessiveness and look at those causes and not the weight itself.

As with everything there is a root cause, trigger point and reason for any excess behaviour. That does not mean it is not my fault and cannot do anything about it, that it is all down to someone else to correct but seeing that the problem exists themselves - that is the first step on the way to recovery. To ask themselves, What problem do I have that necessitates comforting. What is it in my life that needs attention, which needs nourishing with comfort, and in some cases - food?

Everything that is excessive is out of balance to the natural rhythm of the body, what it was designed for and what it is able to consume and do. The more natural the product as in unprocessed and untampered with, is the most natural for our bodies and the easiest to digest. When we get indigestion for instance or heartburn it is our bodies letting us know that what we have eaten, or something within what we have eaten is not agreeing with us and is having trouble coping with the substance. Our bodies will always naturally let us know if something is out of balance in various ways, just as when we hurt ourselves or cut ourselves, it sends us a signal to let us know so that we can remedy the situation in whatever way is necessary. The same with our bodies when there is an imbalance it will let us know in whichever way it can.

Not always straightforward as sometimes it is complex and may have many causes, which are not obvious to the recipient. Because the causes are so varied, it is sometimes necessary to ask for help, albeit a doctor, friend, counsellor or in whatever seems appropriate to the person concerned.

Causes can come from various areas of one's life, it could be a concern you have about something you are not confronting or at least sharing with someone. It could be from some emotional turmoil of some kind in a relationship, concerns for other people that really do not concern you, a worry from a parental aspect, monetary concerns, where you are living – hundreds or even thousands of different reasons could be the cause. Whatever is the cause, it needs to be let out in some way, it needs an outlet and not to be locked within, where it can fester and the cause of many imbalances. Emotional turmoil or even diseases and ailments of many kinds, if left over many years can cause no end of damage, which sometimes can lead to an early death or a very serious disease indeed.

It is for us to take responsibility for our own health and general well-being, for us to choose wisely what we put on and into our bodies and for us to deal with and face what it is that is indeed ailing us in whatever form that feels appropriate for us at the time. There are many occasions when it has been left too long or needs immediate attention. Perhaps an operation would be necessary to cut out a diseased portion of the body or urgent medical attention needed in another form, an alternative or natural therapist to aid the healing or some other form of help.

It is always to be aware that after such treatment or help has been sought or deemed necessary, that the cause of the ailment still needs to be addressed even though the symptoms have been dealt with. It is the cause of the ailment that has not been treated and often can return in the same ailment at a later date or in fact form and hinder in another way.

All causes need to be dealt with at the core of the problem; they will not go away of their own accord. It is for us to take the responsibility and deal with it once we have realised where it has initiated from. It could be something that is recent and not voiced to the person you have issues with, also issues from way back somewhere in your past that have been left there to fester, not dealt with and now when it has grown out of all proportions, reared up and taken the form that it has.

There are exceptions as I said earlier; there are in fact cases where people have chosen to leave their bodily form in the manner of a terminal disease of some kind. Which may seem unbelievable to you but we all leave this earthly plane in a variety of ways, when it is appropriate for our spirit to move on. There is a vast difference from people who go this way through choice and having the experience from a spiritual point of view, to those who are suffering in some way through a lack of self-denial and fear that confrontation of any kind would be a fruitless task, or do not wish to face what needs to be dealt with or do not wish to upset those around them in some way.

I say this now to you in all honesty, your life is your responsibility. You come (usually) into this human experience on your own and almost certainly leave in the same fashion. What you make of your life and experience here is totally up to you and no one else. It matters not what others think or in fact what they say or do.

This life is of your own making to live your life through your heart and not your head. Living a life of honesty, one of balance, one of commitment, faith and courage to be all you can be – life without end.

For this is your total reason for being here on this planet, to grow as a spirit in whatever form it takes and whatever circumstances you are brought up in. They were your choice for the experience and lessons you came to learn in this lifetime, make no mistake about it.

This is it, part of your life's cycle, part of what you came here to do and be. A part, a fragment of the whole and here to learn and move on from whatever went before.

PART OF THE WHOLE

Each one of us is a fragment as I have said before – yes, a mere fragment but an important fragment just the same, each playing our own individual roles, each of us unique in our own ways, none of us more important than the rest, each of us playing an important and unique role in the overall scheme of things. A part of which is so vast, so magnificent, so powerful and yet so beautiful at the same time, a cosmos full of all the imaginable and not so imaginable and more. A universe full of energies, without structure, and without a direction until it is given one.

We are the direction, not only us but all spirits of the universe.

Why is it that man sees itself as being the overall Supreme Being when it cannot even cope with the planet it is inhabiting. Ever mindful of some other far-off galaxy, ever mindful of where else it could be and how much better off it would be, doing anything other than what was intended. Spending billions to find answers to things that are already here and around us, spending billions to research cures and answers when they are already there within and cost nothing except of course for a little ingenuity, courage and faith to be different.

The courage to admit mistakes, the courage to lead the way into a united and compassionate way of living together as a whole of this wonderful planet of ours.

When I say ours, it is not ours at all. In fact nothing is ours, it is all borrowed it is all on loan, nothing goes with us except all that we have learnt along the way from what we came here to do, be and experience.

This is what is important, not how clever we think we can be, not how much we feel we have accumulated along the way.

Hasn't anything been learned from what has gone previously?

Did the Pharos take all their treasures with them? And did not the people pilfering their graves and tombstones learn the lesson there also intended for them at that time?

We see ourselves as supreme beings, well most of us think that way don't they? Yet we have come such a small way from our very beginnings.

Okay I know this will stir a lot of people up, but before you go beating on my door, please just give it a few moments thought and ponder please on what has just been written.

Have schools and education moved on from the past 50 years or so? Except that a few of the lessons have changed and they now have computers, instead of having to think or work things out for themselves.

Are they taught to use the skills that they naturally have and were born with?

Are they encouraged to pursue their dreams? Are they supported both in the school and in the home to the ends that are most suitable and of interest to them, or is it more to the case of what fits into society best for the others and the easiest solution and easiest route taken.

These children are the future of this planet and although there is some work being done in this direction, there is an enormous amount of work and change to do.

Where does the money come from? I hear you say, from the billions that are being spent unnecessarily and to what ends?

You may well get an answer (cure) to cancer, the same as the answer (cure) to other problems and diseases that have gone before. It will make no difference, for as one disease is cured the ailments and diseases that people have, will just take another form. For it is not an answer, it is not 'the answer'. It is as I said, for each of us to take responsibility for who and what we are, to be responsible and ask more questions about everything and not just leave it to some others to do and think it has nothing to do with them, for it has everything to do with each one of us.

Has the quality of our lives improved? I don't think so. We race around in ever decreasing circles doing, doing, doing.

Are we all happier?

I do not see it on people's faces or in society as a whole; I do not see it in the faces of teenagers, who are quite often at a loss of where to go and what to do.

There are areas that are improving and some people go to great lengths to help, but it needs a major shift, a major move not just from certain individuals but from us all as a whole.

Nations, governments, society as a whole, not a case of it is nothing to do with us, as it is society's responsibility all of us working as a whole, working together to bring it about and a change in our attitude and perspective to such issues.

These problems will not just go away, they have a cause like everything else, a need to listen to what is needed, a need to listen, instead of – you shall do as you are told!

It has never worked and will never work. Because the more you restrain and deny people of anything the more they will rebel and work against you or society in general. It is to live in cooperation and assist each other in any way we can and look always to the cause of any problems, whether it be social, emotional, personal to you or some illness or malaise.

Whatever it is, there will always be a cause and it is to address the cause, so the imbalance can be addressed and rectified.

It is for the good of us all, it is in all our interests to do so and to do so with haste before we cause any more damage to ourselves and this planet.

We need now to take responsibility for all our actions, each one of us in whatever way we can. Taking the lead, showing what can be achieved and making a difference, not only in the lives each of us live but a positive difference to the planet, the result will be a spin-off from all our actions. Whether it be in thought, action or deed, it all makes a difference EVERYTHING POSITIVE DOES.

But hey! It is not all gloom and doom, it is also good for us to be able to enjoy our lives to the full whilst being aware and more conscious in our actions. There is so much here for us all to enjoy, it is all around us in abundance and is purely our choice of how we wish to view the planet and our lives. Whether we wish to look at life through a positive perspective or whether we wish to see many things around us as negative and best to be avoided at all costs!!

It is of your choosing, it is for you to decide for positive thoughts bring positive actions and therefore positive results. Where the negative outlook only brings more doom and gloom, a heaviness now that needs to be shaken off and a fresh new approach to life and people, one of compassion, friendliness and openness would be of great benefit to all.

There is abundance of everything for all as I have already said. I'm not saying equality for all, as that would never work as there always needs to be degrees of everything but more of a balance, more of a balance between haves and have not's.

There is no need in this world for anyone to be without a roof over their heads or to go hungry no matter what their situation, colour, creed, race or religion. It is for us all to bring this about in whatever way is possible.

So let us put an end to all that has gone before, for it is all just memory, some of it of a very painful nature but memory nonetheless. One for us to learn from, accept it as such and move on from, not to be repeated over and over again. To look at our history and all that it has shown us in past lessons, past lives. It's not this moment nor the future but pure memory, one to be moved on from in a positive and fruitful manner.

Amen

BEING MINDFUL

Our natural state is spirit and it is of utmost importance to remember that in our everyday lives, for what we are and what we are being not only affects us in our short time here but in our future lives and indeed for all eternity. Something we should all ponder on and remember as we go about our daily lives.

Do unto others as you would have them do to you, would be a great attitude to have. One that would bring about so many wonderful changes, it would take so little, just a thought, a kind gesture, a moment of compassion or kindness, for you never know when you yourself are going to walk a similar path.

Indeed you never know, what you will need to learn from this lifetime's experiences because it is not only your choice of what you choose to do and be in your next lifetime but also to learn from the consequences of this lifetime's endeavours. For what goes round comes around. At some point in time, when that moment is appropriate and when the spirit is ready to learn the lesson involved.

It would be wise to always be mindful of this fact, for it is very true. So be mindful of your actions, even of the smallest nature, even to taking a parking place that was not yours!

There is no such thing as a coincidence; no such thing as an action without a reaction EVERYTHING COUNTS and everything is taken into account.

That is why I say to you BE MINDFUL and be compassionate to people who may well be having a hard time, as you cannot have any idea of what has gone before or the lessons they have come here to learn. It is not for us to judge. Judge not, least yea be judged, for in your judgment will bring a reaction and a judgment on you and your actions.

It may seem complex, but it is in fact very simple, as every action has a reaction, totally everything we think, say or do. It is not that someone is looking over you and deciding what you are doing and whether it is right or wrong, good or bad as there is no such thing. Only what works and what does not.

You are the masters of your own destiny, you have complete free will to do and be as you please BUT everything you do has a reaction, whether it is good, bad or in between. It is natural order of the cosmos, if you like; you draw in and give out positivity or negativity and you attract like for like. To put it another way, what you are being you are seeing, in every sense of the word.

A question of focus on all you would like to do and be in this world. A focus at all times on your goal in question and along the way, taking steps in line with reaching that goal. You may need to sidestep, you may even have to do many things that you do not enjoy doing to achieve this, but along the way the opportunities will be there to guide you and to steer you if you maintain that focus. It is not always easy, and the path that leads you there is often a bumpy ride, but if you have the courage, faith and the belief in your own convictions then it is impossible to fail.

A belief in yourself and all you are doing and being that is the answer, if there is such a thing. Because really there are no answers to anything, for as soon as you feel you are getting close to an answer the goalposts will shift and the direction to that answer will be a different one.

There are only questions, not answers and it is for us to question everything. Question all we are doing and all we are being.

Is what you are doing or being, really you?

Does it fit; does it feel comfortable to you?

Is it really who you are?

For in each of us is a unique spark, one of creativity, one of uniqueness, an eternal being, a clear light, bright pure being of such magnitude, one of joy, love and peace.

It is all there in each of us - yes everyone, yet some of us choose to ignore it and go a different way. One that can only bring misery and grief until they decide to choose differently, as everyone does in the end.

How many lifetimes that may take is up to the individual spirit. It can choose differently in the next second or nanosecond if it so chooses. So you see it is all a matter of choice, one of discernment one of our own choosing.

We all know deep down in our hearts, right from wrong; we all know but some of us have forgotten. Forgotten who we really are, forgotten that we are spirits and I can only describe it best as, being asleep. Have blanked out any remembrance of who they really are.

Sometimes it is something they have come to learn and experience and sometimes it is easier to go with what they have been brought up with and easier to keep going down that path, than to wake up to the fact that it does not have to be that way at all for them. It can indeed be very very different, and until they realise this and wake up to the fact that they can change and take the necessary steps to do so, there is nothing much anyone can do, except by showing them that there is a different way, a different way of living and being. Showing the way through example.

It is often the case that they have never known or seen another way, so how are they expected to know or do anything different.

When you have seen and experienced better, you do better.

Over the generations it has come to pass that more is better, that the quality of life and indeed everything is of little importance.

QUALITY IS EVERYTHING; expect the best and you will receive the best, to accept anything less is to deny yourself, your spirit of who you truly are.

What you wear, what you eat, where you go and what you do is an indication of who you are being at that time. Indeed it changes with the circumstances of the moment, but generally speaking, what you are wearing and what you are doing is portraying to the world, who you are. It is also an indication of how you are feeling within too; to be somber and withdraw is shutting yourself away from your life and what is immediately around you.

To be smiling and upbeat is to portray a picture to the world of your brightness and your inwardly happy feeling, one that is infectious and encourages others to do likewise.

So much black has entered our lives, not only in the clothes we wear but in commercial premises, shop facades and in many items that we buy for some reason now come generally in black. It is usually a draining somber colour, which does nothing for our spirit; and does nothing to embrace any colour or brightness into our lives. Yet if you look at nature, look at trees, plants and flowers they are full of colour. You will rarely find black amongst them, unless of course we have tampered with nature and tried to make it something it is not.

So, why I wonder?

I can only presume that is the general mood and feeling of doom and gloom that is portrayed around us, both in the media, business and indeed ourselves and how we view the world around us.

The same with quality too, so much of our products seem to have taken a downward trend in quality. Making quantity instead of quality the main focus. We have only ourselves to blame there for it is purely a case of supply and demand, to be more discerning over our purchases; for if we did not buy them they would no longer exist.

It is quite simple and straightforward, if you want a better quality of life, better food in our shops and better health, then we need to be more discerning over our choices. Your body is a living-breathing organ of course – you would not be here otherwise! Its needs to be nurtured and cared for, otherwise it will break down. There is no point continually giving it processed foods and then wondering why it ails you or gives you problems in one area or another. It needs protein in various forms, it needs natural unadulterated foods, ones that are as close to their natural state, just as your body is.

I am baffled as to why people are surprised at the rate of various diseases and illnesses that are on the increase. Your body can only get its nourishment from what you consume and if it is fed continually food, which is unnatural to it, and food that it was never designed to function with – then something has to give!

It is not always obvious at the time, because the body tries to cope as well as it can with what it is given, in the end though over a time and with a buildup of chemicals and toxins that the foods contain in various forms, it gets to a point that it can no longer cope.

A question of self-love in many cases, a feeling of self-worth and who and what you think you are. We are all deserving of better, not only of better but the best that we can afford at the time.

In many cases, the weekly food expenditure comes way down the list of priorities when it comes to monthly or weekly spending, when really it should be the most important expenditure of them all. Foods that are fresh, full of vitamins, full of colour, vitality and are as natural as one can get.

If you do not enjoy good health, you miss out on so much or sometimes all the things you would like to do. There is no better feeling than having a body that enjoys good health and is full of vigour, you deserve the best not only for your body's sake but for those immediately around you too.

A time of discernment in every area of one's life, a time of choosing wisely if you wish to have a better quality of life and see quality coming back into our shops.

It is in your hands, it is in all our hands for what we choose determines our future in every sense.

A QUESTION OF CHOICE

This book will not appeal to everyone, because what I am writing about and suggesting takes effort and not everyone will be wanting or willing to do what it takes to change their lives around, but for those who do, there will be many benefits in all areas of their lives. Some small, some life changing, depending on how far you wish to journey down this route.

All I can say is; it is one of self-discovery, doing and being who you truly are, bringing your lives back into balance with all that is natural around you and all that you were intended to be. A far cry, from what the world is in general today.

This does not mean stepping out or away from all you have known or all that you enjoy in your life but to enhance it and bring about positive changes.

For some of you the changes will be more radical than others, some may find that there are only certain areas they wish to concentrate on, but any changes however small can only have a positive outcome.

A journey of discovery, one of self love for if you cannot love yourself, this unique beautiful being who can you love?

You were born out of love and loved you will always be; if not by yourself, then by the universe, who knows nothing but love.

It is not selfish to love yourself, as this is your natural state. To love yourself who you are and your uniqueness in this world is one of the greatest gifts that you can give yourself.

You were born perfect as you were meant to be, not always perfect in the physical sense but perfect for the role you came to play, perfect for what you came to do and be. There are times when there are imperfections of a harsh nature, but all are meant to be for some reason or another, some to show others the way of compassion, some to learn from previous lifetimes.

It is complex and we will never have all the answers; that is not what is intended, it would only hamper our growth and make something finite, which you will never be. You cannot expect something, which is growing and expanding constantly to be finite. It is a never ending journey one of expansion and creativity – world without end.

So it is for us to embrace this fact, embrace all that we see around us. Because one day we will have learnt to love unconditionally.

Unconditional love – has no boundaries, no barriers, no must do's – no judgment, nothing, just total love for who and what we are.

If we choose it to be a drudgery then so be it, but what a shame and what a waste of all that we could be, do and enjoy.

All down to us, our choices and how we wish to perceive this wonderful world of ours. A speck in the universe, a fragment of the whole, only a fragment but an important fragment nonetheless as I have said before.

People have prayed to God to come and save us, but save us from what? Ourselves?

You cannot have total unconditional love and then put conditions and limitations on that. It is as it is, and is for us to do something about what we feel is not right in this world, to bring about changes we would like to see. Down to each one of us, focusing on a positive bright future and doing what each of us can do to bring about these changes in whatever way we can; in our homes, in our surroundings, in what we portray to others and how we treat ourselves too, all with love and kindness.

How do we bring about changes and how can we see a bright future, when most of what we see and hear is doom and gloom?

See the positive side to everything, as there always is one. If you live in a mostly closed in space, make time to go to a park, river or stream or the sea if you are close enough. Be as close to nature and anything natural that you can be. Think positive thoughts, focus on what you would like to change about your life, then take positive steps in that direction.

When buying something to wear, always buy something that you love, NOT something that you think will do for now or see something at a slightly higher price and dismiss it even though you love it because it costs you a little more. Down to how much money you have? Sometimes, but in most cases not; it is better surely to buy one good quality item that you love, than buy three or four which are mediocre and you think will do.

The items you love, you will keep and treasure, those you do not will quite often sit in the cupboard or closet unused and unloved, because they were a choice not made from the heart but from your head and lack of self-love and what you deserve.

I have often seen people saying how much they would love something and then choose something less expensive, not out of necessity but because they for some reason think they shouldn't or feel they have to justify buying it, to themselves or someone else. Self-love, self-love – too many should's and ought to's. Too many self-limitations on what you think you ought to do and be instead of pleasing yourself, being happy about who you are, what you are doing and what you are being. Too caught up in what others think and may think of you – it is none of their concern – not unless they are the ones paying of course and as long as you are not causing any one grief. Even then it's up to you to be discerning and buying what you love, not what you think you ought to get.

It is how you wish to portray yourself to the world and also a question of what makes you feel good. To wear an item of clothing that you love, I feel lifts you and gives you such a feeling of self-worth.

All a matter about caring and being conscious of everything you do. Not only that but going with what resonates with you.

It depends so much on the changes that you wish to make for one to suggest generally the steps to take, as it is an individual choice, as each of our journeys and paths are so different.

A focus is the main thing, focusing on what it is you would like to change, and taking positive steps in that direction. Most of us know how to bring about positive change in our lives and sometimes it takes a little pre-programming of the mind! Breaking old habits, breaking new ground, a little discipline perhaps, a little or a lot of effort and occasionally, courage.

All or some of these are necessary to bring about change – it is easier in some ways to just go along with the flow and just put up with the way your life is, but in the end it is change that makes life worthwhile, if you are not happy with the way it is. I am not saying change for the sake of change, but change if you are discontent or unhappy and need to take certain steps to improve your situation.

Life and the cosmos are all about change and is changing constantly and we need to change with it. Not to constantly live life in the past, looking back over our shoulders, hanging on to what has been, gone and past, but one of constantly replenishing and recycling just as nature does, as we are part of nature and it a part of us, both dependent on each other, for life and nourishment.

If the change you are wishing to make seems too daunting a task, take small steps and do it gradually until you feel ready and comfortable with what you are trying to achieve. Small steps are better than taking no steps at all. Each of us has our own comfort zone where we feel happy to be. There are times though when these thresholds need to be crossed, to push out boundaries and invite new experiences, people or things into our lives. Stepping out of comfort zone enables us to grow and move on to even greater things than we have already achieved. We have all achieved many many things; even being born into this world was an achievement. It took courage, strength and a huge leap of faith, hoping there would be someone at the other end to love us and care for us. So surely pushing out of you comfort zone or even taking down barriers whether it be to people or experiences we would love to be part of can only be a good thing.

In many ways it is all part of our journey to explore the unknown to us and forever expand our boundaries in any way that we can. For life is intended to be an adventure, one that leads us ever nearer to who we really are, peeling back the layers until we discover the truth about ourselves.

This can be achieved more successfully when time is taken out to be by oneself in the physical sense. When you are on your own you have to think yourself, fend for yourself, make your own decisions about what you are going to do next, but when you are with a partner or friend it is usually a joint decision and often not one you would make of your own choosing if there was no one else there. To be on your own some of the time gives you the space to listen to your inner guidance, one that comes from your soul, the part of your spirit that is guiding you or trying to guide you along your previously chosen path for this lifetime and all your lifetimes.

If you take the time to listen, it will not usually be a voice, although it has been known to many but a feeling or instinct, on which direction to go or what to do next. Sometimes something will come to mind that you had not previously thought about, you may have an unexpected encounter with someone you have not seen for some time. Whatever it is will always, well nearly always have a better chance of happening when you are on your own physically.

I say physically, for no one is ever truly on their own; it just seems that way sometimes. Your spirit is always there ready to give you a helping hand in whatever way it can, in a practical sense. It is for us to ensure that we have some quiet moments to ourselves, so this connection can be made more clear to you. It is always there though, even when you are not on your own.

I wonder really how many people give a thought to where their ideas and instincts come from.

It is not from your brain that is sure, as that is purely a device, a computer to store knowledge that has been acquired over time. Something you have learnt and somewhere where memory is stored, to remind you in the future of certain things that may be useful to you at a later date. To remind you of previous experiences good and bad (although nothing is good or bad, only your perception of such things, that is all). You may feel that some experiences are not of a good nature, but after a while when you look back on the incident or the bad experience, you will see there was always a good reason for it being so and sometimes see the reason why it was meant to be, or perhaps you will never know and will never be able to see the reason clearly, especially if it was a traumatic time for you.

It may take years of healing and coming to terms with certain things happening in your lifetime, but as I have said before there is no such thing as a coincidence and there is no such thing as anything happening without a good reason.

So if you are in such a space at the moment, please remember what I said – you are never alone; even though you think so or feel that way or feel that everything is lost, for it never is. Take a few moments without anger, if you can and centre yourself. Take deep breaths and breathe in the life that you are, connect with your spirit and find peace in those moments. They will give you strength, they will give you guidance, it may not even be immediate but it will be there just the same. Something will happen, something will guide you to a place of comfort, if you let it.

Thankfully, not all moments are like these, we have wonderful memories even wonderful memories of people who were dear to us that have moved on, either at an early age or of later on in years. Wonderful moments there to be cherished not to be relived time and time again in our minds but ones is to be loved and cherished for the moments that were truly wonderful.

Gifts that will always be remembered with love, which is always the best way to remember such times, even when something you may think is dreadful at the time, for everything that is past is memory and is best left at that and seen for what it is. As spirits come and go when they choose for one reason or another, mostly unknown to us, and it is not for us to reason why, for it is their choice and their life's journey whether it be here for a few years, months or live to be a right old age in our terms.

Being here is such a small part of our existence in the bigger scheme of things, it is purely a blip in our time as a spirit.

Sometimes it is hard for us to understand this and want to take revenge in some way for what seems to be lost or done to you, but there is never anything done to you, it is all part of your journey and what you came here to experience. One of letting go, moving on and seeing it for what it is if you can; as one of life's experiences, sometimes of a wonderful nature, sometimes not.

Some people have everything fall into the laps from a very early age. It is their journey this time round and they are here to learn completely different lessons. I cannot stress enough how this journey we are on is purely transient, although of course it will not seem so from a human viewpoint. A very complex journey yet simple in many respects. One of evolvement on the spiritual level.

We may feel that these people have a wonderful gifted life and live like princesses or kings, but I say to you now, you have no knowing of what they had to do or what their previous lifetimes entailed.

So judge not if you can, for all is NOT as it seems, only in your mind's eye.

It is your view that you have at this moment from a human perspective and not from the spirit that you are, that is unless you have travelled down that path and see life here on earth, from the spiritual perspective and not the human one.

It is for us in some way to find hidden depths, to delve deep until we find our reason for being here. To find out just as much as we can from what we are doing and who we are being whilst here in our embodiment. To do this is to grow, not only from a human perspective but to grow and expand as a spirit to, for when we leave this mortal place called Earth, all our knowledge from books or anything else will be of little consequence.

It will be what we have acquired from our experiences here, what we have learnt in the way of wisdom and an understanding of others, and the way we have coped on our journey. In the way we have handled the situations we were given and the way in all honesty, we were loving and kind to others.

These are the true gifts and ones that will live with you eternally.

ROUND IN CIRCLES

In the beginning was the word and in the end silence – very apt indeed, as our natural state is silence!

So to have constant noise can drown out our natural ability to receive guidance. In fact some people use noise and constant chatter or some other means such as never stopping to have a moments relaxation. Always being on the go, busying themselves to stop the buzzing in their heads, which is trying to get them to slow down!

The lack of slowing down or the lack of relaxation is a vex in this world. Constantly always doing, having to be on the go at all costs. In fact at all costs, is usually what it is because it costs dearly both to our mental state and to bodily functions – it is called STRESS, a condition, which is usually self inflicted and one that usually stems from a constant doing.

To be constantly doing is not to be BEING, and being is your natural state, one of BEING in a relaxed state.

Stress causes all kinds of illnesses and diseases; the body cannot cope with such things over a great period of time. It can only lead to malfunctions of all kinds in the body, its organs and nervous system and has a very damaging effect on our self-esteem. For we pretend, we wear masks, pretending all is wonderful to everyone we meet and in most instances, it works. It is a covering up of who you really are, a covering up and a running away from yourself. Not wanting to address what it needs to be sorted in your life, not wanting to come to terms with certain issues, that are of paramount importance. Sometimes being all everyone else wants you to be and not being YOU. Shutting out that screaming voice in your head to STOP take a moment have a rest, relax, it is SO important!!

It is somewhat rife in this world, where there seems to be little time for anything or anyone. Peddling faster and faster on that treadmill until you are exhausted from it all – having to take a holiday – then back to repeat it all over again. Rushing from one place to the next, always in a constant hurry. Why? Timescales, jobs to be done, a meeting to go to. Would really a minute or two either way really make that much difference? For you though that little bit of extra time would make ALL the difference.

I can assure you it was never intended and we only have ourselves to blame. Forever, wanting more and more of something, anything to fill our time and our lives, and for what? Things? Perhaps, I am not sure.

Eventually, everything comes full circle whether you wish it to or not, and whether you break out of that circle or expand that circle is entirely in your hands and no one else's. You cannot blame anyone else for your circumstances, you cannot say 'I would have done, if so and so had not happened to me'. Nothing happens to you, it is what you bring about and into your life.

Not always the case but mainly it is,. It is the choices that you make that determines your future and the experiences that you have. Some are contrived and from a choice made from the spiritual state. They are your lessons of this life.

How can you tell the difference between the choices and the lessons?

The best way I can help you there, is by the experiences that keep repeating themselves over and over again, until you have grasped what is intended and then when grasped and acknowledged, then used. It is not learnt until you have made it part of your life and part of your learning experiences. It is not enough to say that, 'I am never going to do that again' and then at some later date repeating the same thing – whatever that might be.

It may be something really small to you, seem quite insignificant or something quite major that repeats itself, until you are so tired of it happening, you take steps never to do it again!

Yes quite an uphill struggle sometimes, but it is the same for everyone, regardless of status, age, colour or religion. You see it is the same for everyone, even though it may not seem that way from your particular life or viewpoint. There are no favoured few, the rules if you like are the same for us all, just the circumstances of our lives are different.

All intended to be different that is why everything is unique and individual, can you imagine the world if everything was the same;

How would we cope without any variety?

Police identification parades would be a farce

Fingerprints would all be the same

Passport photographs would be pointless

Everybody would be of equal intelligence and have the same skills

We would presumably have to have a number tattooed on our foreheads, who would control the numbering system throughout the world?

Buying clothes would be simple, all the same size and shape

What criteria would we use to select a husband or wife?

Watching a film would be really tricky

No more recognising someone we had seen years ago, unless we remembered their serial number

I figured there must be some form of universal intelligence, which recognised these problems and ensured that each and every thing is different.

So you see everything has a reason for being as it is and everything has a specific reason for being as it is. There is no reason for us to meddle with anything or try to change anything. EVERYTHING was made perfect for its own form and function, perfect in its own way, whether we agree to it being this way is another matter. Surely it would be far more beneficial to us as a whole, to work with such a wonderful ingenious universe that it is. To enhance its beauty, to enhance its ways of being, rather than to attempt to destroy or alter in any way. In doing so only upsets the balance of nature and the world, it takes away the reason for being as it is. A wonderful diverse universe, one that has provided everything that we need in abundance, one that has given us life, one that has nourished and cherished us since time began.

A love that transcends any other, as I say whether we wish to see it that way, is another matter entirely.

To use what is readily available is the key, to use what nature has provided for us in its natural form.

Somehow we need to retrace some of our steps, rediscover some of the lost ways of our past that were more in keeping with our natural state, our natural way of being. Bringing those up-to-date and working alongside them in our modern everyday lives, along with all the other technological advancements.

Not to cut out all that is natural to us, not to think we can survive on chemicals and something quite alien both to us and our body systems that we were never designed or intended to absorb such substances.

There are certain times when chemicals are the only answer in an emergency to overcome a certain disease or ailment, but only as a quick temporary fix when the ailment has reached epic proportions and huge doses of drugs are really the only answer.

The natural way is a gentle way one that is not obtrusive in any way to the body, one that was provided for us by nature, one that is in tune with our physicality and our spirits. These are intended though to take at the onset of any ailment, when the condition is treatable from the very beginning, when the body is a little out of sorts and not functioning on all cylinders. Which of course was always the intention, for everything has always been provided in abundance, it is just sometimes our mismanagement, use and indeed overall consumption of all that has been provided, which has been abused.

So many of the way things are now on the planet are of our own doing. Yes there is climate change but that has always been the case since time began, it may be a little exaggerated now through the misuse of all that we have been given. It is for us now to be more responsible, reduce our expenditure in the way of resources and work with the planet and nature in a way that will benefit all.

You cannot keep emptying the vessel without putting something back. A case of balance in every degree, a case of adjustment and realignment, a massive effort is needed to bring all this about and quickly, otherwise there will be an overdraft that will never be able to be repaid, not without thousands of years going past anyway. People and governments need to put a stop to what is going on around them; no specifics as people know who and what it is. Too much greed, too much trying to please other people all the time, instead of getting the job done.

A rethink of our commitment to life and the planet, a rethink of all we are doing and being.

There is some change going on, but alas it is still all too small and all too slow. It needs a major shift of conscience, a major shift of our priorities each and every one of us and not left to just a few people to do, wanting to shield ourselves from the truths and hoping it will all go away.

IT WILL NOT ALL GO AWAY, THAT IS DEFINITE!

We seem to be happy just going from day to day not questioning anything, and in fact not even wanting to know at all unless it encroaches our doorstep and we are faced with an ultimatum, then and only then, do we seem to make a stand.

We think it is there just for us to use and quite often abuse, and this has been the case now over many generations. You only have to look back over the past few decades to see how much has changed, some for the good but unfortunately mostly not.

It can be done, as I say; I would not be writing this to you otherwise.

A little like bringing a naughty child to task, often kicking and screaming and if necessary this will be the case – let's hope not for all our sakes, our children and their children too, for there is much to be grateful for, much to celebrate in this wonderful world.

FLOW OF ENERGIES

A time to work and a time to play, a time to be and not to be, a question of when to and when not to. Sounds like a riddle?

No not really, simply a matter of flow, a flow of the energies that are all around you and within, using them to your best advantage, knowing when to and when not to.

A feeling, timing – let me explain.

We live in a world that is full of energies, (mind you, everything is energy – but that is for another time) a little like the tides, they come and go. Sometimes high, sometimes low but always there in varying degrees. Some are useful to us, some are not and it is in this distinguishing between them that can make a huge difference to the functioning of our lives on a daily basis.

To know when to pursue something and when to let it go, can be a great advantage. For instance, when you wish to do something and it all seems such a struggle. You try everything to make it work but somehow it just does not want to. Sound familiar?

Well that is when to leave it alone, drop it go on to something else, it is not right for you and is giving you a hard time so that you will do just that – let it go!

You can of course continue with your painful efforts and in doing so the energies in the end will give, but you can be rest assured it will not be a pleasant experience what you insisted on doing and will sometimes work against you in an extraordinary manner. This does not only relate in things that you wish to do, it could be anything from a purchase, a holiday, an event, a house purchase, even in a relationship of every kind.

It is all there for you and if you work with it will benefit you in many ways and save you from a lot of agony!

Whereas if something is meant to be and the energy flow for them is good, you'll know instantly the opportunity or event will almost jump out at you wanting to be taken up and used. It will go smoothly and effortlessly, be a joy and a good or wonderful experience.

In the purchase of something too, just the same, if it is readily available, if it is the colour of your choosing, if it fits perfectly (well most of the time) and as soon as you put it on, you love what you are seeing and it makes you feel good, then purchase it, love it, it will be good to you and for you.

The same goes when you have a job or chores to do, not always so simple because sometimes you have timescales and there is nothing else for it but to knuckle down and get it done! But if you do have the opportunity and have a choice of when to do it, then it is always better to do it at the moment – it feels right. It will be done much quicker, far easier and smoother if you can go with the flow of energies than work against what is and what is not working for you, at the time.

Energies are constantly changing; so what will be appropriate today may well not be appropriate tomorrow. Something that would not work today could well just fall into place easily tomorrow.

All a matter of energies and also a case of timing too, for everything – even this book I am writing.

Something I wanted to do and complete last year not this, but for some reason or another it would not work, one thing after another got in its way. I had to wait for the right moment and the right timing. Not only for me you see, but the right time for it to be out there. The right time for humanity and enough people who need it and would appreciate its content and be able to use it.

A matter of timing, not just a matter when you want to get something done or completed. It takes a little patience and a little getting used to but works beautifully – if you let it.

Life is not meant to be a chore; there is everything there to help you along your path and journey in life. Your experiences to and the opportunities that come along for you, just at the right time that is perfect for you and your chosen life.

Everything in your life has led you to where you are now. All the choices and decisions made along the way are all part of who you are now, a whole conglomeration of experiences, choices, things or opportunities, some ignored.

Everything has brought you to this moment of now, for now is all there is and ever will be. Yesterday is but a memory and tomorrow, well we know not yet.

You may have it mapped out, you may have had it planned up to a year ago, but fate if you like, has a habit of changing things at the last minute, throwing a spanner in the works or indeed throwing in one or two pleasant surprises.

In fact the more you plan your life and day to the last detail (some people do), the less chance there is for spontaneity to come into play. Spontaneity being flexibility, one that can lead you down a wonderful path of exploration, one that perhaps you had not considered before; again it could be anything because it is your life and your life's path that determines these moments of joy.

To be open to such moments needs flexibility in one's days and one's plans; a sudden change of direction, a sudden impulse or inclination can sometimes change your life around or at least point you in a direction not previously thought of.

It can still happen even if your day is fixed, when you are at work for instance. Even then you can choose to take your breaks differently, or do something different in your lunch break. Perhaps if you intend doing the family shopping then, do it differently sometimes if you can. Go to the park if there is one, go for walk instead, make time and a few moments for you. It will all still get done – try it – you will feel the benefits almost immediately.

Spontaneity – yes, it is a matter of being open to doing something different at a moment's notice, being willing to try something different, being open to change – what life is all about. Being, ready to jump, if that's what you need to do.

Having a feeling for what is right for you and not dismissing it out of hand, because it seems somewhat different to what you would normally do. Having a little courage to let fate take you down a slightly different or sometimes totally different path to what you are doing or experiencing now.

Just because you are heading in one particular direction does not mean you have to continue down that same road. There is a whole world out there to be discovered, a whole host of opportunities of all kinds.

So come on now - what is it you would like to do or be?

Give it a chance, let it take you by the hand and lead you on a wonderful journey of discovery, one that is open to all – yes all – in our different and unique ways.

The continual flow and change of energy is there to help you and lead you to where you need to be. Choosing the moment that is right for you, one that is of your choosing one that feels right for you and is open to you – not warding you off, you will know from the signs you get. You will know from your own feelings whether or not it is right for you.

The reason I keep writing 'right' is because really there is no right or wrong, only in our own minds. It is down to what works and what does not, plain and simple. If it works then continue to go with it, if it doesn't then let it go - leave it alone. THAT GOES FOR EVERYTHING!

Where to go to, what to do – its a feeling – a feeling from the heart, not the head, a feeling – a knowing what is right for you what you think will work and what will not.

To procrastinate and to go over it time and time again in your mind is unnecessary, to think it through for a few moments is all it takes. It is your first impression your first instinct of something which is usually the one you. To go over and over something in your mind only complicates the issue and that's when insecurities and doubts of what you are about to do creep in. That is when quite often opportunities or changes of some kind get put on the back shelf, when in fact they were ready and waiting for you at the moment of conception, the moment of first thought, followed by action.

As I said previously, is not always easy to change course or alter the direction of your life but a very worthwhile one, a part of your journey, a part of what you came here to do. To deny such instances or deny such opportunities is to deny self, to deny the real person that is you.

Some people have made massive changes, when being made redundant and suddenly find there is a whole new world out there. A day that had never been thought about, seeing it before as something others do and not themselves.

Some see it as a release from what they had always known, looking at the redundancy as a golden opportunity to do and be different, explore other avenues of occupation, taking a change of direction completely and going on courses or retraining in some other occupation. Sometimes people are forced into different directions through necessity and found other avenues opening up for them along the way, for others it could be a bereavement that brings about massive changes, a total rethink about their lives and sometimes their homes and even location comes into play.

It is different for everyone every time, as to the ways the means and the circumstances, but always to be viewed if possible in a positive and productive way. One that releases you from the past, one that lets you determine your future by the choices you make at that moment in time.

Everything is a precious gift sent to help you and to guide you on your way. One that sometimes strips you to the core, a feeling of rawness of vulnerability, of pain, grief and sometimes suffering in some way but nonetheless a gift. These things heal – well not always entirely, but sufficiently enough for you to pick yourself up and move on.

Move onto something that is 'right' for you in whatever way presents itself to you and whatever way feels appropriate.

Sometimes it takes another's ideas or experiences to bring change about, one of positivity and growth, one that works and has been proven to work by their own experiences along the way. Through trial and error, success and failure, grief and hardship, traumas of various kinds.

All worked through, all seen for what they were and stepped through the other side triumphant and glorious, both in the physical and the spiritual path that is life.

Energies, yes everything is energy. Everything you see is energy, resonating at such a speed as to make it solid, a different pace for different things depending what they are – I find that totally incredible.

Even more incredible is all that we don't see. For example; as in the space around us. The air is also energy and in fact has far more energy in it than the solid matter! Molecules and atoms that are invisible to the naked eye, unless you have a gift in this area as some people do, who can see energies, auras around people, objects and plants.

In fact we all have the natural gift to see all these things, it is just a matter of training our minds to accept them, study the so-called spaces and seeing the wonder within those spaces.

That is all I will go into on the subject, as there are many books available, which will lead you in this direction and show you how with a little training, and a little belief 'in all that is', is all that is required.

Nothing has changed in the world's energies that we use or could see, it is just that until recently it has always been seen to be, far out there and not for use in our daily lives.

For generations and long before, certain countries have been using what has always been available to them. Many books have been written on the subjects but here I am hoping to simplify its uses, so we can move on, evolve and grow into ourselves and all we came here to be. To bring it into our daily lives where the energies can be understood more and used more, as they are readily available to all and completely free.

Nothing is needed to use these, no prayers, or medication necessary just an acceptance that they are there.

You use mobile phones, televisions every day without a thought of the energies that transmit those messages through the airways, so why not use the other kinds of energies to enhance the way you live and work. The more you use them and the more you get used to them through practice will soon have you knowing instinctively when and when not to do something, it will have you listening more to the guidance that is readily available to you and will have great benefits to your health too.

Listening to your body, adhering to its warnings when it is hungry or just thirsty. Knowing when a certain food is needed and when it is not, when the food agrees with you and when it does not. All signals, all instincts and tuning in to all that is around you and available to you in different ways and in different forms. So much to do, so much to be and this lifetime to make a difference in ourselves, and all that is around us.

Many will say that it is impossible or even undesirable to connect with something that you cannot even see, but as I have said before you do it every day of your life unconsciously. To be conscious of your thoughts and actions will bring you immense benefits of all kinds. You will learn to be more aware of everything around you. Realise that things that are not meant to be will be hard or almost impossible to manifest. And then suddenly when the time is right the way will become open to you.

It's all a matter of trust and to go with the flow of 'all that is', knowing that a much higher and more intelligent power is guiding you, nurturing you towards something that will benefit you greatly in the long run. To be at peace with what is at this present time is the secret, but to also have a focus on what ultimately you would like to do and be. Leave the details to the universe and know that it is all in hand. Opportunities, ideas and people will come into your life when the time is right. Believe it and trust it, it will serve you well. Moreover be true to yourself in every respect. Be aware in all you say and do, being anything else is not who you are and will not help you at all on your journey.

SHOULD'S AND OUGHT TO'S

Baggage - everyone has baggage, so they say.

I think it comes from those who have a mass of baggage and cannot come to terms with dealing with any of it, letting it go or seeing it for what it is.

Baggage can come in many guises; it is amassed from experiences in our lives that we thought gave us trauma of some kind, and as small children when we take on board anything we are told as absolute truth. Then there are the experiences through adolescence, all of which if not dealt with at the time are stored and filed away as memory, which can at some later date be triggered by a similar incident and then seen in the same light.

It is called baggage, I think because it is something that weighs you down, causes untold stress and can even add on unwanted pounds in weight' which will not shift it seems, no matter what you do.

Memory that's all it is, but by us is seen as something that has to be carried around for the whole of your lifetime. Not so - it needs a change of perspective, a change of attitude and purely a searching of and dealing with whatever issues are causing the baggage in your life.

It certainly is a good name for it, because it is heavy and weighs heavy on both your body and mind, making it at times difficult to deal with and can cause anxieties of all kinds.

It's almost like a clearing of a cupboard or attic that has been left undisturbed for a long time, one of those jobs that keeps being put off until another time and quite often, that other time can be put off indefinitely. Not a good idea.

All these past issues or dramas locked up in the closet need sorting at some stage, and the sooner you can face doing it and sorting some of it out, the better. It just takes, normally, a little courage and effort; often to write letters to people to vex your feelings about some past issues you had, or just getting it down on paper how you feel about certain things that are giving you anxiety. You may not even know or be able to link an issue or anxiety to a past experience, as it will be so stored away under a pile of other issues that it will take some time to unearth it and bring it out into the open. You may not even be aware of any issues that you have stored away and feel that all is fine and dandy, but there will be times and some trigger points somewhere down the line to remind you. A call or email from a certain person you do not wish to deal with, a relationship that is nearing its natural saturation point and you are unwilling to let it go. Certain moments of doing or seeing someone, because someone else wants you to but really if you had your choice would not at all - but you always have a choice.

Do you see what I am getting at?

There are no should's or ought to's in this world only in your own mind.

There are times of course, when you do things for other people out of love – that is completely different and it is done with love and kindness,. A realisation that they just are, as they are, and are not someone you would normally associate with but you do so as I say from a place of loving not from a place of having to.

It is doing things that are going against who and what you are, doing things that you REALLY do not wish to do that cause a buildup of resentments, and over time they can build up into something out of all proportion.

Sometimes doing too many things for other people and not even realising you are doing it can cause issues of a bodily nature, from carrying extra weight 'baggage', to stomach upsets or even headaches. An imbalance that needs to be addressed, unless of course you wish to carry on the same way; not take care of yourself and love who and what you are and being.

A matter of choice but not a healthy one if you wish to continue down the road of self-denial, and that is all it is. A total disregard of self, a lack of self loving of who and what you are, a lack in interest of your own journey and what you came on this planet to achieve, do and be. Some people focus totally on other people and their lives, getting totally absorbed into what they are doing and being, so wrapped up in fact that they lose all sight of themselves.

Quite often it is a way of focusing away from their own lives and issues that they would rather not deal with or face, so they focus and do for other people instead – constantly.

If they are happy to do this so be it, but they are not really helping those people in relation to their journeys, for all it is doing mostly is to help them out, prop them up and deny them their lessons and what they came here to learn also, as they are not moving on in their own journeys and what they came here to do.

It may seem harsh to many people, and it is not intended this way and hopefully you can resonate with what I have just written and see it for what it is

It does NOT mean not helping people out or lending a hand whenever you can, that is not what is meant or intended but a balance, a healthy balance of when to and when not to and the circumstances to which you are helping. For there is no substitute for kindness, kindness in word thought or deed most of the time. I say this, as there are occasions when your own boundaries are tested and then you may have to vent your feelings, but there is no reason why this cannot be done in a controlled and civilised fashion.

Look at young children – they don't have baggage. They do not hold back on their feelings about anything.

We have a lot to learn from them, they see things as they are and if they don't like it they say so – end of story. No buildup of resentments, no buildup of issues, it's out there in the open, usually done and dealt with in under ten minutes or so, then forgotten and moved on.

Wonderful how they make the most complicated issues to us seem so easy and straightforward and they are, it's only us who have problems with doing so. Just our timing of such things sometimes has to be a little more appropriate that's all, everything done, sorted and moved on from, so that there is nothing left to fester and multiply.

Oh what a different world it would be if that were so, no more arguing or squabbling going on for weeks, years or even generations. All sorted, all out in the open, all our energies focused on the future, our future and what we can do to make it a better place for all mankind. Not just in our own country or on our own doorstep but throughout the world, a concerted effort by all – how wonderful that would be.

It is all about unity and comradeship. Being open, honest and above all living in a natural healthy environment. One that builds on and supports our bodily immune system and not deplete it, as so many things that we take or absorb on this planet do, it is our immune systems that keep us healthy.

Of all the wonders in nature the immune system must surely rank as one of the greatest, without it we would be at the mercy of every germ and virus going, and yet we abuse it in so many ways. We all know that it is able to adapt and learn how to overcome disease, and the stronger we make it the more effective it becomes, just like a muscle, if not use frequently it will become flabby and ineffective.

There are two certain ways to weaken our immune systems; firstly, excessive stress and secondly, the use of drugs. Stress causes severe imbalances in our system, reducing the effectiveness of the immune system, this is all too clear to see by the number of colds and bugs we pick up when we feel low or run down.

The solution most of us opt for is to seek help from medical science and take the latest wonder drug or antibiotic, which at first sight appears to be the answer to everything in the way of health care.

This is not the case, as all we have done is send the message to our immune system that it was not needed. It fails to produce the antidote for the ailment and is unable to arm itself for a return of that particular strain of virus, because it has been weakened by the drugs given.

The immune system plays a vital part in our wellbeing. It would be well to remember that when we feed it insufficient nutrients or take drugs, it slows down its efficiency and sometimes disables it completely in extreme cases, where continued use of drugs and chemicals have been taken.

It is for us to be responsible for our own health and well being, to do what is necessary to bring this about in the way we eat, exercise and take care of our bodies in every sense. They are a highly tuned and sensitive organ and put up with all sorts of abuses from us at times. To love and cherish your body is to love who you are, as it is part of your totality. A part that was designed for you to play and be the part you came to be in the journey called life.

Everything you have been given in your physicality was meant to be, each part of you divine and indeed perfect for your role. For loving it is loving you, and if treated with loving care will give you many years of service. Not only in what you eat or the exercise taken but what you put on to your face and bodies as everything is absorbed through the skin and into your bloodstream.

Also taking life at a more leisurely pace, making time for relaxation and moments of peace; not only when away on holiday but as a foundation to the way you live and work. Not only is it essential to the body, it is essential to your mental and spiritual states that plays such a huge part on whether or not your life is a healthy one or not.

Stress is one of the biggest killers of mankind in the physical sense. It produces huge numbers of toxins in your body, which left over a considerable time, grow accumulate and causes all sorts of diseases and bodily ailments.

It is pointless going to the medical profession for a fix, if you continue going down the same route after you had been fixed! For these things do not go a way of their own accord, they have no outlet, they have nowhere to go, unless you release them through being kinder to yourself, changing your lifestyle and fixing the issues at the core.

The medical profession can only treat your symptoms, it is for you and no one else to treat the problem that you have, from a willingness to accept, first – that you have a problem and then secondly taking steps to face and deal with whatever it is that is causing the malaise. Once willing to accept responsibility and seeing your problems for what they are, an imbalance within – however caused, then and only then, can you seek a road to recovery. How?

There are many options open to you, depending where the problem or problems lie, you may need outside assistance of some kind. Ask openly in your mind guidance, direction will always come, if you are open to suggestions, open minded enough to find a natural remedy, one that is in keeping with your ailment. It will be there for you. A sudden idea, an inspiration, an advertisement in a magazine, a chance encounter with someone who knows someone. It will be there waiting for you, if you are willing and make the effort that is required.

Yes everything takes effort; otherwise there would be no point or purpose to anything.

Everything that you do in your day takes effort and the rewards in doing so far outweigh the effort involved.

Isn't your life and your body precious to you?

Isn't it worth the little extra time it takes to be more conscious of what it is you need to do, to make your life a happy and healthy one?

A healthy mind leads to a healthy body; I have heard it said, which is absolutely true. That from your thinking comes the doing; from your thoughts come the actions and the reactions.

Many say it is in your genes how you are, and that is true to a point, it is the foundation of who you are and is part of your chosen journey what you came here to learn and experience. It is from this foundation that you grow, but there is nothing to say that you cannot change that very foundation. Build yourself a new one and decide to be different, decide it is not for you and gradually change the structure to something that feels more fitting and comfortable.

Changing your life and your very foundation is mostly to do with your thought patterns. How you see your life progressing, how you view your relationship to your parents and how you perceive yourself to be as a person.

It matters not what has been and passed, it matters not what ailments your family have. It is more to do with how you feel about yourself and your relationship to this that matters most. Your journey and life on this planet are about you. Not meaning that everything else falls by the wayside, far from it, it is about you and how you relate to others and how you relate to yourself. Your general outgoing persona to the world and what you contribute to it.

Now that is what matters!

A far cry from, do as I do; because it all depends what that doing is! Whether it fits in with you comfortably or not, and whether or not you wish to follow that path and direction, or whether choosing your own way in life is the better option.

All down to options, choosing, and what you choose to do and be that makes your journey and makes your life's experience.

A bit like a computer game, choosing your options and with those options taken – the outcome of the game.

That really is the easiest way to describe it, it may seem all too simple. In fact life is simple, it is only us that complicate things. It is not always simple to carry through the options and sometimes extremely difficult and challenging to do but he sense of achievement once accomplished, far outweighs any of the hurdles that were there to negotiate.

Being true to yourself and following your inner guidance, is the key. Not a practical thought out plan, not one of; when we get to such and such an age or retirement we will do, so and so, but an involvement of life from the very onset. Participating in life, facing all its many challenges and hurdles and also to grasp opportunities that come your way that feel in keeping with your journey and one takes you further along the path of your chosen journey.

Your dream, your focus and all it is that you would love to do and achieve in this lifetime, your journey here on earth.

A wonderful life and challenge, if you are willing and open to it, have the courage and commitment of your intentions and actions.

All this and more can be achieved without the necessity of being unkind or cruel to others, without the need for an ego trip as so many people do, but as a commitment to self, to you and your journey. To honour others too in the same way and know that each of us is on our own journey and what is right for you may not fit into another plans, in any shape or form.

It is for us to honour that in each of us, to step into our role with love and kindness, with truth, dignity and above all – yes I repeat – kindness. Nothing beats love and kindness towards another human being, regardless of what you think they are or might have done. To remember that each of us is on our own chosen journey to learn the lessons of previous lifetimes and also to learn what we have chosen to learn from this visit here. We have absolutely no idea what they are or what each of our journeys entails.

That is why I say, focus on what you need to do and be and a little less concern over others and what you think they should or should not be doing.

Be a role model, be a wonderful example to the world to follow, for to shine your 'light' brightly; quite often enables others, to do likewise.

If each of us were to recognise this fact, and be a participant in life, instead of an onlooker, many of life's problems would disappear overnight. People would feel part of the whole, which indeed they are instead of being segregated, separate or singled out as different or somehow strange. None of us are strange or different, only the colour of our skins and the language we speak is different, giving each of us our own uniqueness that nothing else can.

A uniqueness that spans the globe not only in the human species, but in everything you come across that is alive, living and breathing on this earth – including all vegetation.

So perhaps a little thought into the perceptions and feelings of others, for sometimes it is not always as it appears to be from the outward appearance, in fact most times it is not at all how it appears to be but something quite different.

An accumulation of events and experiences that brought you to this moment of now. This moment of being who you are and for you to decide whether you like the outcome or not, and if not what steps you are going to take to remedy what it is that is either painful for you or what it is that ails you or feels uncomfortable in your life. Something new that needs to be brought into it or something that you have outgrown that needs discarding.

A far cry from what has been in today's terms; a far cry from what there is to come if we persist in journeying down the same road that we are now on.

As I have already said, change will come and it will be of our own doing and making, it is for us now EACH OF US to choose what way that is to be. One of separateness and disfigurement, or one of unity and self-love. Knowing that we are ALL ONE, each part, each one of us being a fragment of the whole.

To acknowledge that fact and live as one, in tolerance and kindness towards each other, knowing that each one of us has their own journey, albeit long, short or totally different from our own.

We may not even know it or acknowledge it, but nonetheless it is so. Always has been always will be, it is only our perception and separateness that encourages us to think and act as we do.

A time of change, time of commitment to what we can really do and be. A time to be thankful for all we have and all we do.

A time of consolidation in our everyday thoughts and activities in whatever direction that may take us.

Choose well; choose carefully, for what you choose today, shapes yours and our futures for tomorrow.

ABOUT THE AUTHOR

A person who has a great affinity with people and the problems they face in this ever demanding world. One who has experienced so many of lifes challenges both physically and emotionally, has found ways to overcome these and written this book to help others in a practical and easy to understand way.

Having worked with people on a one to one basis in a natural health clinic for many years. Gaining experience and insights into the ways of the universe and now shares this wisdom with the world.